Stolen Snapshots'
by "Drift Away" pe

MW01232574

["Fantastic Foreword" = the place where someone famous and influential to the author says really cool and wonderful things about the author and/or book. It comes at the beginning of the book and takes up this page.]

"Give me the beat boys to free my soul...
I want to get lost in your rock & roll and drift away."
— *Drift Away* by Mentor Williams
[as performed by Dobie Gray]

If, as the song says, love is lovelier the second time around, the same holds true with reading Zork's *Stolen Snapshots* the second time around. I'm a stickler for gleaning little gems that I may have missed the first time through.

I found myself guffawing without reservation at the acumen with which Eric [a.k.a. Zork] demonstrates his wit. And, as I read the passages that could only have come from deep within a sensitive soul, that indescribable *something* kept tugging at my heartstrings.

I am delighted to have been asked to add my two cents to the blurbs in Zork's book. Here's hoping that all who read these words can hear the beat and really free their soul.

From strength, to strength,

– Dobie Gray
– Performer *Drift Away* (1973) – w/ Uncle Kracker (2002)

Stolen Snapshots' Brilliant Backword by Manhunter co-star Tom Noonan

["Brilliant Backword" = this is the place immediately behind the "Fantastic Foreword" where a favorite famous, fantastic and certainly sarcastic celebrity & character actor writes something really clever. (And Zork reminds everyone that "Manhunter,*" directed by Michael Mann, is by far the best of the* "Silence of the Lambs*" series... thanks much to Tom & Mr. Mann).]*

"As part of an out of court settlement, the details of which I am not at liberty to comment on, I have agreed to 'endorse' this book by Eric Zork Alan. I can only recommend to all those who come in contact either in person or by telephony with Mr. E.Z. Alan to record all pertinent conversations."

– Tom Noonan
– Actor: *Manhunter*, *Knockaround Guys*, *The Pledge*, *Heat*
– Writer/Director: *What Happened Was*, *The Wife*

[1991] Zork & Mr. Tom Noonan on the set of *Monsters*
[otherwise known as *Tales from The Darkside*
with a completely silly name change]

Stolen Snapshots Book Blurbs

[This is where the author and publisher have famous, cool and/or respected people say very impressive things about the author. Remarkably enough, Mr. Alan did not even have to pay these people.]

"Zork's collection is madness; sheer madness, but take the dive, sort through the oysters, find the pearls... they're there."

- *Roger Bonair-Agard [performance poet]*
- *1999 National Poetry Slam Champion*
- *appearances on Russell Simmons' Def Poetry Jam [HBO], 60 Minutes, Charlie Rose*

"Whether he is delivering a riotous rant, a satirical stream of consciousness, or a lavish lyric, Zork is so often over the edge that you quickly become attuned to the free fall of his words, and find yourself eagerly awaiting the next flight of his imagination, enjoying the sentiment of his heart so blatantly poured out in line after line. Zork is as original a poetic voice as I have heard in years."

- *Faith Vicinanza [poet, teacher, editor, publisher, and director of The Connecticut Poetry Festival]*
- *Publisher: Hanover Press, The CT Poet, The Underwood Review*

"Zork's book is a Romantic's manifesto that covers every stage of a modern relationship. The first meeting, the "Oh sh*t! This is the one!" feeling, the first kiss, first sexual experience, the less clumsy sexual experiences that follow, and finally the "oh sh*t, this isn't the one" feeling.

People who have their "stuff" together and know ALL the ins and outs of love, don't need this book. But if you are a human with a squishy heart that has the net to catch love but no cage to keep it, '*Stolen Snapshots*' will let you know you are not alone and give some guidelines on what to do....and what NOT to do."

- *Yolanda Wilkinson [performance poet]*
- *VH-1 Slam Champion; Member of national finalist NYC/Union Square 2000 National poetry slam team*

"To truly experience Zork in all his 'majesty,' you must really see him in the flesh (but hopefully not too much flesh). But if you cannot make it to one of the Westchester County hot spots where he routinely works his magic then *Stolen Snapshots* will give you a sense of what he's all about. Just remember to read the pieces as Zork would have. By which I mean, read them while lying on the floor, standing on a chair, or while handing out copies of pictures of himself with famous people to total strangers… stuff like that."

- *Richard G. Lewis [lead bass player]*
- *Sam Black Church [Boston, Mass.]*

"I am flattered that Eric values my opinion more highly than three of the original four Monkees. I unreservedly stress that this volume is second only to the *American Science & Surplus* catalogue in its power to class-up your coffee table, nightstand, or bathroom vanity."

- *Andy Ihnatko [Columnist]*
- *Chicago Sun Times, MacWorld Magazine*

"I have three words of advice: Buy Zork's book. It is a much smarter idea than going for Danish in the FRONT seat with Joe Pesci in the back with an ice pick. If you get my *point* you will buy *Stolen Snapshots* and then sit in the BACK seat with Pesci!"

- *Chuck Low [actor]*
- *Goodfellas (Morrie); The Mission (Cabeza), Sleepers, etc.*

"Zork's poetry is honest and fresh. He evokes dreams & memories of love, of first kisses, of shared passion, of separation, of change and of the thrill of falling in love again and again. Relive your journey through his unique stories & style... you will find yourself in his book. If you are out of love, you will find a way to get back in. If you are in love, you will fall farther."

- *Deb Snyder [actress]*
- *Star: Ang Lee's Pushing Hands [his 2nd best film... rent it now]*

"Unlike any other poetry I've read, *Stolen Snapshots* stimulates this sort-of hungry voyeurism . This book is so completely ZORK, out there, playing full-out, self-expression untamed. I open it up, begin reading, and keep reading and keep reading. I just love such conquest."

- *Marj Hahne [performance poet]*

"From the first time I watched Zork hand out Pop Tarts during his reading to a poetry audience in Westchester, I knew he was not one of our traditional 'garden variety' poets. His poems, like Pop art, call attention to the relationship between the ordinary and the extraordinary in our daily lives. The author himself says it best '*Zork, it's not just a name, it's a way of life!!*' Grab a Pop Tart, a margarita, a copy of *Stolen Snaphots* and get ***Zorked!***"

- *Cindy Beer-Fouhy [Literary Arts Director]*
- *Northern Westchester Center for the Arts*

"Zork has an original voice, a different way of seeing things. He has true passion. I think every young person should read this book, as it is an authentic yearning that is true of 'Everyman' who is honest with himself."

- *Gerard Brooker [poet]*
- *A Quiet Conversation [A Wing and a Prayer Press]*

Steve Buscemi politely declined to blurb this book [through his people]. We think he has absolutely no recollection of Zork. [see p. 68]

Photo by Bill Decker [1990]

Stolen Snapshots

[I am not a poet]

By

Eric Zork Alan

www.zorky.com
www.stolensnapshots.com
poetry@stolensnapshots.com

This is not your parent's poetry!

[and don't ever forget... *Everyone* is a poet!]

ISBN: 0-9724111-4-3

Library of Congress Control Number: 2002094

This book is printed on acid free paper.

First Edition

Edited by Heather Ostman

Open Mic poems featuring Colette D'Antona,
Deborah Nicolai Heller, Megan Buckley & Isabell Yiskos

Alliterative Authors Press
21 Branch Brook Rd. • White Plains, NY 10605 • USA

Alliterative Authors Press-rev. 02/24/03 [435]

Why should you buy this book?

Well, if you had been one of the first 5,000 people to email a poem to submit9@stolensnapshots.com then you might have been handed this book for *free*.

But since you weren't that quick you should understand poets *should* be paid for their prose.

Please buy this book to support the arts and help me recoup the losses from my insane 5,000 book give-a-way. I can then go and get back my appliances from the pawn shop.

My mother told me it was a really silly idea (but still she loves me and my work and lets me visit home to steal leftovers from the fridge).

Lastly, because poetry never does pay, you can all feel free to hire me at my properly premium priced Macintosh consulting rate to fix your computers.
[*Free* book with 1st consulting service]

Poetry doesn't pay… computer consulting does. [consulting@zorky.com]

The world needs one (or more) less starving artist.

Why Macintosh?

Well, to be blunt, is there any other computer that an artist would work with!?

This book was created entirely on a Macintosh G4 with OS X, Adobe Photoshop, Microsoft Word, and Adobe InDesign.

Steve Jobs [co-founder of Apple computer] gets a free book [even without submitting a poem]. "Drop me a line, Steve, and I will hook you up."

Have I mentioned that my MACnificent Macintosh services are for hire? consulting@zorky.com .

You ARE a poet!

[even if you don't *know* it yet]

Stolen Snapshots: Open Mic Project

Everyone is a poet and has *something* to say. But people are [often] too afraid to put it all down and *share* it.

Stolen Snapshots: Open Mic [Alliterative Authors Press next publication] will be all about *poetry by and for the people.*

Stolen Snapshots: Open Mic will feature poems from previously *unpublished people.* Bankers with more than statements to say, accountants with rants about tax codes, teenagers with angst about their age, elderly individuals who just realized that *now* would be a good time to write a love poem to their long loved spouse. Even your mother can probably pen a poem [and please do take out the garbage].

Soooo, an important element of *Stolen Snapshots: I am NOT a poet* is to show you that I did it. I did it so much that after a year of doing it I was touring and featuring as a performance poet and writing this book.

So now it is *your* turn. Use the form to the right and/or go to the web site and show me something sappy, sad, or silly. Or even really romantic. Anything at all.

Through this book [and its related promotions] I will collect 5,000+ poems from *unpublished* people. A hundred [or more] selected submitted poems will be subsequently published in *Stolen Snapshots: Open Mic.* Please help this project to breed more poets, submit a piece of your heart today!

Thanks for sharing,

Eric Zork Alan
poetry@stolensnapshots.com
www.stolensnapshots.com

[Several pages of this book prototype "Stolen Snapshots: Open Mic"*]*

Open Mic Poem Submission

[Entry implicitly agrees to allow Eric Zork Alan and/or Alliterative Authors Press to publish (without reimbursement) the associated poem. The author agrees to *NON*-exclusive publishing rights in any Alliterative Authors Press publication. This means, if you get famous from a *Stolen Snapshots* book you still can publish your poem *elsewhere* for a fortune.]

I understand/ agree signature [sign here to submit and let Zork profiteer from your brilliance and poem… see other side for all details]		Book#:
Name:		
Email:		
Phone# [optional]:		
Vocation:		
Age / Sex:		
Favorite Poet:		
How many poems have you written / published?:		
When did you write your first poem?:		
What was your first poem about?:		
Why do you write poetry [in 10 words of less]		

Mail to: Alliterative Authors Press / 21 Branch Brook Rd. / White Plains, NY 10605

Open Mic Submission
Legal Mumbo Jumbo Page

[Submitters cannot ask Zork or Alliterative Authors Press for any money if any *Stolen Snapshots* book becomes a *New York Times* bestseller. Zork will be very lucky to break even after giving away [trading] the first five thousand copies.

Instead of a mumbo-jumbo page, this is where Mr. Alan *should* admit he was a bit wacko with that poetry trade thing.

Anyhow, please fill out the flip side and attach a poem and mail it to:

Submissions #9
Alliterative Authors Press
21 Branch Brook Rd. / Suite 609
White Plains, NY 10605

Please *also* submit your poem [if possible] via the web site [hopefully you are using a Mac] at www.stolensnapshots.com [click *submit* link].

If your book is numbered on the flip side of this page then please make sure you enter that number in the SUBMIT form.

If you can't submit via web site, then please also email poem to submit9@stolensnapshots.com .

Thank you for submitting your poem; it makes Mr. Alan feel less crazy when *other* people share their sentiments via poetry.

We are not all here alone!

Stolen Contents:

Endearing Acknowledgments:

The poets: Faith Vicinanza, Bram Lewis, Mike Robin, Mar Walker, Alice-Anne Bridgers, Dot Antoniades, Reggie Marra, Jen Murphy, Suzy Lamson, "profess" Kevin Burns, Raul Maldonado, Pamela107 and all the Bethel Arts Junction and Hudson Valley Poets.

My models: Debbie Rochon, Dave Mattey, Colette D'Antona, H Linton, Traci Mann, Liz Ross, Judy Johnson, Matt Brighton, NewHire, Ken Brickman, Chris Oldi, Sarah Moreau, Leslie Hardie, Maribeth Cummings, Sharon Paige, Doug Sakman, Melissa, Scott Harris, Lizzie Phelps and "the box."

… and, of course, my muses: the Brazilian, Delicious Dell, the Talented Teacher-Lady, Indy, the AmazingActress, the GermanGirl, Kuzy, Acting Amanda, MaureenB, the sexy Special K Lady, KimC for frequent flower miles, Luscious Leslie [who *almost* won on *Jeopardy]*, TinaM 4 intriguing me , L'Artiste Lady, the puzzling lawyer who I lost before we contracted our first kiss, and the 6' nurse who would have been tall enough if only the romance weren't so short.

IreneIreneIrene Tejaratchi… it was the very best kiss I ever shared… you know you will never be any less than 3 * Irene, 3 * a lady, and 3 * my love.

Jen, you taught me how much my heart could love at 13 while roller skating without brakes. And while "*muskrat love*" may end, my love never will. "*Endless Love*" is always on my radio.

Also, my cover girl, MagnificentMollyMeg who is short and sexy and sometimes too smart for her own good. Hopefully she will soon remember to think less and enjoy magnificent moments more. She knows how to reach me with a smile and a kiss.

I would have liked to love her less, because falling can hurt. But it was worth it all for the 10,000 photos, 10,001 kisses, the shared sexy smiles and the sensation of losing my center of gravity. Let's K.I.S.S. some more sometime soon.

And, most importantly, thanks to H, my one and only guaranteed reader. You made me a poet [of sorts] and taught me how to smile in iambic from the inside out. I hold many Pop-Tarts in my heart for you.

EA ;)

About the author:

Mr. Alan spent most of his life trying to avoid poetry and other such "foo-foo" things. Then, somehow, in a series of semi-sensuous ways involving PopTarts and onion rings he found romances that had him belching out poetic prose & alliteratively amorous stanzas.

He has been standing on chairs performing poetry on the East Coast for four years… and sometimes he even gets paid for it.

But, for the rent [and because he loves them], he works with Macintoshes and their associated networks. OSX is a tremendous technology.

Mr. Alan alliterates a lot.

Incredible influences:

As many of the book blurbs indicate [by content and creator] I am hugely influenced by passions for music and film. So loads of love goes out to those artists that made me want to become an artist [of sorts] including: Dobie Gray, John Sayles, Spike Lee, Hal Hartley, Kevin Smith, Tom DeCillo, Cameron Crowe, Sam Raimi, Joel & Ethan Coen, Ron Howard, Robin Williams, Steve Martin, J.E. Jones for *Othello*, Douglas Adams 4 42,Vincent Canby, Janet Maslin, Andy Ihnatko, David Pogue, Cary Lu, Van Morrison, John Mellencamp, Billy Joel, Bruce Hornsby and, of course, Cat Stevens… after all, "If you want to sing out, sing out"… thanks to all these [and *many* more] artists that encourage and exemplify expressive enthusiasm.

Special thanks to Kanner of California for ensuring 712 less poets publish.

Please email comments, critical criticisms, compliments, slanders and seductions to:
comments@stolensnapshots.com [www.stolensnapshots.com]

she talks to strangers

[01/25/02 @ 2:15pm]

She talks to strangers
to make them believers

Believers in the sounds
she makes as
she tells a true tale of
kissing the Blarney stone
and eating black and white pudding
in her native homeland

Born and bred
through three generations
on this side of her
make believe
heritage
she'll show you
an Irish girl
that needs to speak
in her native dialect

the one she learned from
late night TV
and repetitions of *The Quiet Man*

She needs to speak to strangers
to make more believers

She needs to talk
to make you believe
you too can read poetry
when you have yet to learn to write

With the song of a siren
she will free you
of your free will
as she envelopes you
in the sensations of her sounds

To listen is to love
and you *will* love her

before you learn her secrets
of making melancholy music from the heartbreaks
of the lovers she has lost along the way

She'll make you believe that
Frank O'Hara is godfather to
her soul
as she sings in the shower
to provide her neighbors with
lullabies

She knows too many people
don't listen
to the songs we all
use to serenade one another

She goes to carnivals
dressed in pastel colors;
serenades sad clowns
because she knows she can make them smile

She motivates mimes to talk to her
because what mime
could resist
breaking down their walls,
forsaking vows of silence,
and singing along
as they listen and
learn to love verbosity for the sake of her sound ❦

Broken English
[05/26/99 @ 11:15am]

from broken hearts
shattered lines 4 u & me
pick me up… let me loose
tie me together with heartless prose
with promises

reassemble my English

Build me an alphabet
a language
help me soften my tongue

Buckets of style
trimmed of grace
trimmed of place
too sharp
too blunt

Paint me a paragraph with edges and consonants
vowels with lean sensuous curves

Show me a sentence of sense

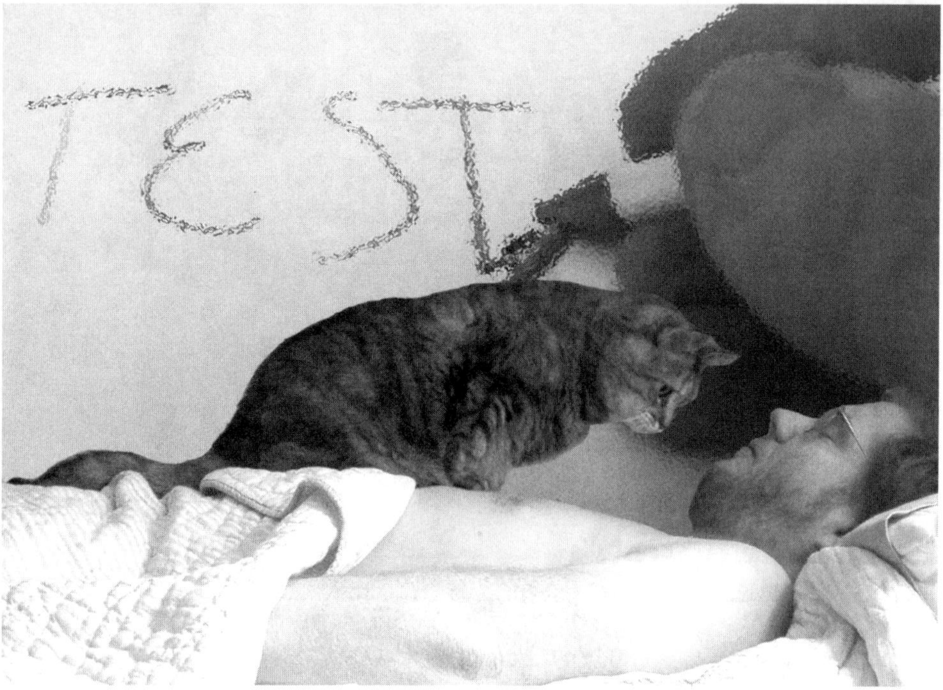

Silent Stutter

[06/12/02 @ 10:00pm]

I st-st-stutter when I say the s-s-simplest things
like *"p-p-perhaps an apple p-p-pie with that?"*
at Mickey Dees as a teenager.

And, tonight, I will stutter,
just the same.

The moment I say *It*,
I will stutter in uncertainty
like buying condoms
at the dime store,
I'll feel the need to put *It* back
on the rack,
hide head and leave.

Or maybe I'll want to pocket *It*,
keep silent,
and steal away.

The moment I first say *It*,
I'll probably cringe
like that first sip
of Bud in the back of McDonald's
at 16.

The first time I say *It*,
my palms will sweat
like when holding an unsharpened number#2
at the SATs
after sequential nights
of sleepless study.

When I first say *It*
I will be short of breath
like after sex
and subsequent spooning

like when I fall asleep,
wake hours later
face up
and face to face
with Chester, your cat,
snoring soundly on my chest,

all 45, or such, suffocating pounds.

[I'll be breathless like *that*
when I say *It*]

When I first say *It*,
I'll think
I'm speeding,
pull myself over
and reach inside my pocket
and ask myself for my license

The moment I first say *It*,
I may stop myself,
stay silent still
… and st-st-stutter ❦

Open MIC

Isabell Yiskos

Arbitrage Broker
Age: 65
Favorite poet: Keats
First Poem: age 6
Poem subject: horses

Why I write poetry:
Is there anything else to do
with spare thoughts?

Play

Jamal paints with green water
on blue paper,
each listless stroke soaking in
as the picture widens into something else:
this sideways house,
this stubby tree.
He can forgive anything.

Each week he gathers the Candyland men
from the four corners of my office.
Red, green, blue, yellow:
he drops them in the stained water.
He holds them down until they are still.

He asks me to erase the chalkboard.
He has a story to draw. ❦

Open MIC

Deborah Nicolai Heller

Actress
Age: I do it well. I do it secretly.
Favorite poet: Edgar Allen Poe
Poems written / published:
Hundreds / 0

First Poem:
@ age 6 about the color pink

Why I write poetry:
I have no choice. I *have* to.

Birthing

Yesterday I sacrificed my prisoner
Drank down life hard
and in a gift of fire
rose the moment
I died
my voice explored
I would listen
as a sacred angel whispered
beauty and truth
are in me. ❦

GAS SALE
I am here

8:47am [aka "I will lie here"]

[09/13/00 @ 11pm]

I will lie here until my erection subsides

until I answer all the questions I have yet to ask
until I am married, father of 2.3, divorced, depressed

I will lie here until my dreams have faded

until I am late for work

until you invade my memory
with lipstick stains

until I breathe your breath and taste your touch

I will lie here until I forgive myself for loving you

until I forget you forgetting me

I will lie here until I have a reason
until gas prices plummet
until I win Lotto
until Cancer is cured
the ozone restored
until politicians have to have smoked pot to run for political office
until the speed limit is raised to 80

until Pop-Tarts and pipedreams are on sale

until I love you again

[I will lie here]

[I will lie here]

[I am here] ❦

And then I kissed her

[07/27/97 @ 3:01am]

We were at that awkward moment. I was not sure what to say or do next.

I had gone to great lengths to make sure I put myself in *exactly* this awkward position.
It was our second date… and the first one that wasn't blind.
I knew there was some interest… I knew we had great conversation.

And I knew exactly what I wanted to do at this very awkward moment.
I wanted to kiss this very beautiful lady, who I was just getting to know, good-night.
For most anyone else this would be a simple thing, a no brainer and something done more out of instinct and habit than anything else.
For me, this is still very difficult.
For seven hours conversation flowed like a waterfall of words. It led us to this

moment of stuttered speech and action.
Could we really have talked for seven hours straight?
I have a mixture of dread, anticipation and an unusual joy… one mixed with much uncertainty.

So we are parked in front of her apartment.
I had gone to great measures to bring my car into the city, something that I normally consider an unnatural act, just so I could drive her home.
Just so I could get trapped in this moment.

She says, *"I would invite you up, but my place is a wreck right now."*

So I will have to make the move down here in the car or outside her door.

We are parked for a few minutes, making small talk that is simply postponing her departure. We are both working our way through this step by stumbling step.

"I should stop babbling and go now," she says.

I will have to make my move soon… I will have to make it *now.*

Only I am trapped behind my seatbelt.

How can I lean over to kiss her when I am still trapped behind my seatbelt?

How can I remove it in a natural fashion without calling attention to my action?

Should I ask her if I can kiss her? Or should I just break free from my seating restraints and be bold?

Should I ask to walk her to her door?

There are so many questions to answer with so little time to resolve them.

There will be no "do over." This will be the first and last time I will have this moment.

She is about to open the door. We are through with the dilly-dallying.

"Would you like me to walk you to your door?" I ask.

She explains that it is not necessary… it is a safe neighborhood.

For a second I feel like I lost an opportunity. For a second I feel like I slipped.

Then she says, *"Unless you want to."*

"I'll walk you to your door... you never know where monsters may lurk in Queens," I say.

So we walk the 30 feet to her doorstep. She has the door partially open and waits. If I don't do something now I will have let the moment slip by. I will miss the chance for our first kiss.

"I would like very much to kiss you goodnight but am afraid of the possible repercussions," I say.

This could be a dangerous lady. So I have to announce my fear.

"Darling, I am too tired to slap anyone," she says.

With the door to her apartment building open just slightly she leans back against it with her head tilted back. She closes her eyes and opens her mouth just a little bit. She waits for my lips.

So here I was at the moment I had worked so hard to find.

I will always remember how beautiful she looked.

I will always remember the simple joy of anticipation.

This was a special moment.

So there she was…

And then I kissed her. ❦

Random filler quotes:

"If it looks like the aim of my kiss is wrong, just feel free to turn your cheek to correct my marksmanship."

"Normally people worry about mice or roaches in the walls, do you always have to worry about horses *in the walls?"*

"Please be specific & guess"

"If we are great lovers then why aren't we being loved now?"

If you are going to do something stupid, you might as well be smart about it. [When giving away 6,000 books of poetry I should have listened to 2nd part of previous sentence.]

CNC Can't

[05/30/2000 @ 8:45am]

Courageous cowardice
can & can't
conduct compulsive comparisons

Negativity
never knowing
not needing

Cancerous coping conflicts constantly
complex caustic caring… costly
costly ❦

corner creatures of public parties

[10/26/02 @ 12:30pm]

This is a poem for all the someones
that feel like strangers
when standing in corners
searching for *something*
to say to *someone*
somewhere in the room

This is the poem for
the private person that
wants to take himself public
even though he has
yet to find his publicist
and has yet to admit
that maybe he *would* like
to mingle with some
of these people
parading around the place
like they have no idea who
this corner standing stranger is

The simple truth is
(from one corner-stander to another)
they don't know who
you are,
and they won't until you make some
sense of what I have to say here

Find a chair and stand on it,
then speak out *loud*

Loudly state that you
love her, that cute one with the curly
blond hair in the
other corner sipping the
banana daiquiri

Surely you will scare her away
… but it won't be from anonymity
It will be from something
more sensational than that

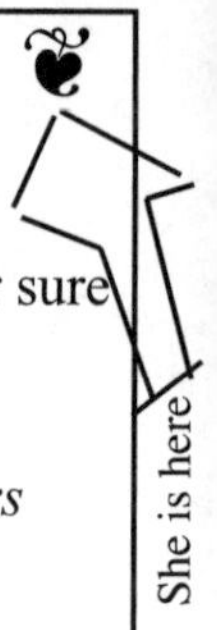

You will now be the
talk of the party

Yes, you will lose this woman for sure
but more from what you say
than what you don't
and that is more than what *matters*
it is what makes you you
and *everyone* else in the room
decidedly *not* you

After all, who else but you would be
cocky enough to stand
on this chair spouting sappy
sentiments to a total stranger?

Are you starting to see what
I am saying here?

Is it starting to make some sense?

But, before you answer me,
make sure you look where
I am standing and clearly
hear that I am certainly not still silent

Susan slipped me a note after
my similar speech
at the Wentz's wedding last week
and I won't be single for long

So, I'll sell you this poem for,
oh, for let's say,
a hundred dollars,
enough for me to take
Susan out
to supper where
I will be anything but silent
in-between kisses

This is a poem for
all those strangers standing
in corners
searching for *something*
to say to *someone*
somewhere in the room

a tie-dyed truth

[11/18/02 @ 10:30am]

Is there an arch needs to be breached
to touch tongue to
palate and then
to say something
other than
"I like you so, so much more
than a lot!"?

What a linguistic leap
to touch tip of tongue
to private parts
of inner mouth and mouth something
other than
"You know, you couldn't get any
groovier
without tie dying yourself"

When on the road,
away from home
I can only ask
"Can I please just CAN you
and call you constantly fresh,
never freeze dried and always
available?

Because you are so much
yummier
than breakfast burritos
on the interstate"

I get stuck saying anything more
sentimentally motivated than.

"You are just so incredibly NEAT
I want only to mess you up some"

or *"You are clearly the number one slot*
on any list Letterman could ever come
to create"

But it's the English
that evades me and
it's been so long since I have spoken
simple things
that I forget
the sound of the sounds
and the syntactical structure
of these sentiments
when said aloud

I forget how to say
to say
to say
that I like you so much more
than like

But I have a desperate need
to tie die you
from top to bottom
to show you what I mean

While still remaining utterly silent
from fear of all that language can do
to make me stumble on my way from
here
to you

Bee Gees Moment

[10/24/98 @ 3:05 am**] [for Maurice]

It's a Bee Gees moment when I want to cry and have forgotten how

Sitting on the window sill
… teardrop raindrops down the sill… down my cheek
… thinking of you
… holding you in memory
… holding you *only* in memory
I ask myself, *how deep is your love, is your love, is your love?*

I remember our kitchen dance…
… dancing… so close… [not close enough]

… right now… *we should be dancing*

It's a Bee Gees moment

Oh, girl, my girl, found and lost girl
I've gotta getta a message to you.
I've gotta getta *my* message to you

You don't know what it's like, you don't know what it's like
to love somebody, to love somebody, the way I love you!

In this Bee Gees moment,
you are so much *more than a woman* to me
'cus every night I lie sleepless with *night fevers*;
the CD player on auto-repeat
making me want to reach out to you even at *the end of the universe*

Baby, you give me *too much heaven*
even when you leave me hotter than hell

Hey, I'd feel *guilty* if I didn't *love you both inside & out*
but instead my *emotions* just leave me with *lonely days and lonely nights*
where I can't stop wishing you would just *run to me,*
whenever you're lonely

I may have *started this joke*... but, as it turns out, I was just *jive talkin'*
whenever I dared to deny it was a *love so right*
yet it did, indeed, *turn out to be so wrong*

Every night it's a Bee Gees moment

If I can't have you
... tears down my cheek
track down, down
into my every
groove ❦

Burroughs' Snooze Alarm

[07/09/01 @ 2:51pm]

My drapes were drippy this morning
as I wiped off the tears

it seems the window washer
has taken a liking to my rear windows
of love lost & fish tanks full of forgotten souls

fishing for the remnants of the paradise I just lost in the night
it occurs to me
that disturbing my sleep
must be part of the wiper's job description

I wake and take a
shower in the sensual melody
of your saliva
draping itself across my Russel-ing passions

I wake and shower myself
with your hands,

the ones you left behind
in the back pockets of yesterday's picnic
on the Charles River

Really,
wouldn't you please come back to me?
your linguini wasn't *that* bad
and maybe I just need to try you out
with a new seasoning or a spice
that I can find in my fridge, if-I-dare

You know you gave me
freezer-burn of the groin
and sometimes I wish I were
a girl, just so I could make you jealous
by coming on to myself in a way you never could

But, all of this thought,
all of these things,
stand before me in my head
on a long check out line only waiting to go down,
down to my last sip

My last sip of coffee

My last sip of coffee

But the *buzz, buzz, buzz* of that bird or bee-
comes under my eyelids with such a fierce aroma

sound scares the window wiper to slip down
and the drapes have all but dried up

they have no coffee to console

But the *buzz, buzz* of that sound, sound

In the shower,
sauntering in your saliva
with only a sip more to go

I succumb to the drips & drops
& spurts
of sorrow

Slash, slash
goes the sound of my sorrows,
swirling down, down my day drains

[buzz, buzz]

"PIPE DOWN!"
I'm trying to concentrate here on the water that is slowly taking control
of my erection & selection of thoughts

I see you looking in through my bathroom window,
checking me out

unlike the window wiper, you are welcome to come
in and take much more than a peek
at what once was the best friend
to all your fantasies
of skiing down my slopes
in our early mornings when you woke me UP
and said:

> *"Hot damn,*
> *I'm horny as hell,*
> *let's finally fuck*
>
> *have sex*
> *in the shower,*
>
> *leave the window open,*
>
> *give the wiper something to work for*
>
> *and come together to sing a bird song*
> *for love lost*
> *and frostbitten feelings"*

[buzz, buzz]

is driving me psycho for sure
while I try to unplug the drain
and slip myself outside into your insides,
or under your arms

I try to unlatch the window,
just as I realize *I don't have a window*
in my bathroom

but *still* I want you inside

me

[buzz, buzz]

Damn birds need to find *my* Hitchcock-
ian ending

Still one sip,
just one sip more

That is when I won't miss you

after one more sip

But, still, I see you outside on my
fantasy-*oops*-fire escape that I don't
have

But, again, and as always, you have
made me so hot,
I must turn into the shower cold

and my morning horn is ready to blow
for you,
if only you would return my favors
with a kiss here
or there

But

[buzz, buzz]

you are not

[buzz, buzz]

you are not

[buzz, buzz]

anywhere

[buzz, buzz]

anywhere

[buzz, buzz]

to be found

[buzz, buzz]

one sip

[buzz, buzz]

just one sip

left

fear of flying

[09/11/02 @ 9am]

I

Afterwards,
I wrap myself with words,
surround myself in their sounds

Not caring to cope,
I alliterate always

Would you rather I rhyme
than use all these "R"s
when refusing to react to this
rotten reality?

I prefer to annoyingly alliterate

I could be working [through this]
with short
sentences
instead

Or silly sestinas
or some such
cerebrally complicated structure

I could be inanely iambic
with a rotten age-old rhythm
forging the frequencies of all
my friggin "F"s

Fuck that!

I fancy a form where "w"s work well
when starting and ending
all my sentences!

Why?

Because, it's what *I* want now

Search out your own silly style
and stop saying my annoying,
aggravating alliteration is so stupid
when it's so ceaseless,
so sequential

Subtlety is a style
that certainly sucks

I prefer the two-by-four technique
when tricks of the telling
are the task of the tongue

Taking care of this craft
and trying to slip out of time today
I've become properly paranoid
of punctuation…

so I don't

period

Instead I exclaim everything
with "E"s,
certainly celebrate "C"s,
sometimes "T"s
But still,
4 syntax,
"S"s make the most sense

Now can u c what I mean?

Today,
how did you structure *your* sentences
into something that made sense
[of this]?

And do you have something to say?

More [or less] than this, that is

II

U c, some 30 years ago
this month
I lost my father
to a failing of his heart
and one year ago,
to this day,
to this hour,
the sky fell
leaving me with
a fear of flying

And sometimes
my heart fails too
in the telling

Instead, sometimes I prefer
to be silly,
do sort of a soft-shoe
with the sounds of "S"s
and smile
like I never knew
what I know now

This poem may be vacuous
and have nothing [serious]
to say
but doesn't
it
all
still
sound
so
pretty? ❦

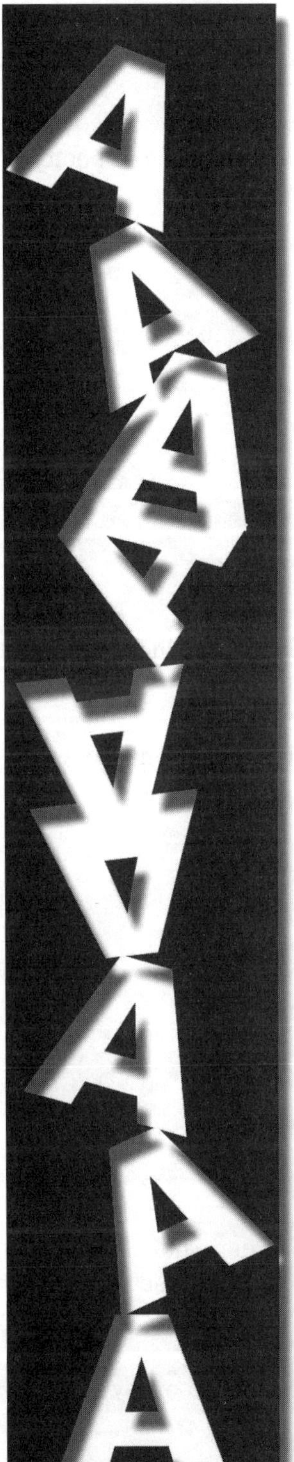

I don't roll the videotape

[week of 03/01/99]

When I get home tonight I won't roll the videotape
because, in memory, I rocked this palace of poetry,
otherwise sometimes known as the house
of the homeless romantics

Here tonight,
I had your souls twisted in with mine
and you smiled
and you screamed
of satisfaction

Moonlighting behind the bar,
I hang and hang loose
and afterwards
I don't roll the videotape
because, in memory, I rocked that roadhouse
I had my words twisted totally into
places of poetic perfection
as I absolutely amazed you with inane anecdotes
and kept your pints poured
and the peanuts plentiful

and we smiled
and we laughed
and I was most certainly never
boring or wanting for words or wit

And all this for some paltry pay
and terrible tips

After we make love,
I don't roll the videotape
because, in memory, I rocked your whole house
I had your body twisted totally with mine

The perfection of my strokes [gesture with hand]
were only exceeded by the perfection of my strokes [pelvic gesture]

and you smiled
and you screamed
of satisfaction

525 lines of vertical resolution doesn't do me justice,
can't do me justice.

After work I don't roll the videotape
because, in memory, I rocked that house
oh, yeah, I showed up on time, left late
made no personal calls,
made at least twice as many widgets as the next worker would
... if only he tried less hard

Hell, I deserve a raise
but I'm not getting paid
so I don't roll the videotape.

In memory, you see, I am quite perfect
we are quite perfect
so don't roll the videotape
do I make myself crystal clear?

There is no need to be totally Trinitron
instead, be totally true to THIS time
and
clap,
laugh,
smile
and come back for some more

Always remember how perfect we can be
we *all* can be
how perfect we *all* can be
how perfect when we don't
roll the videotape ❦

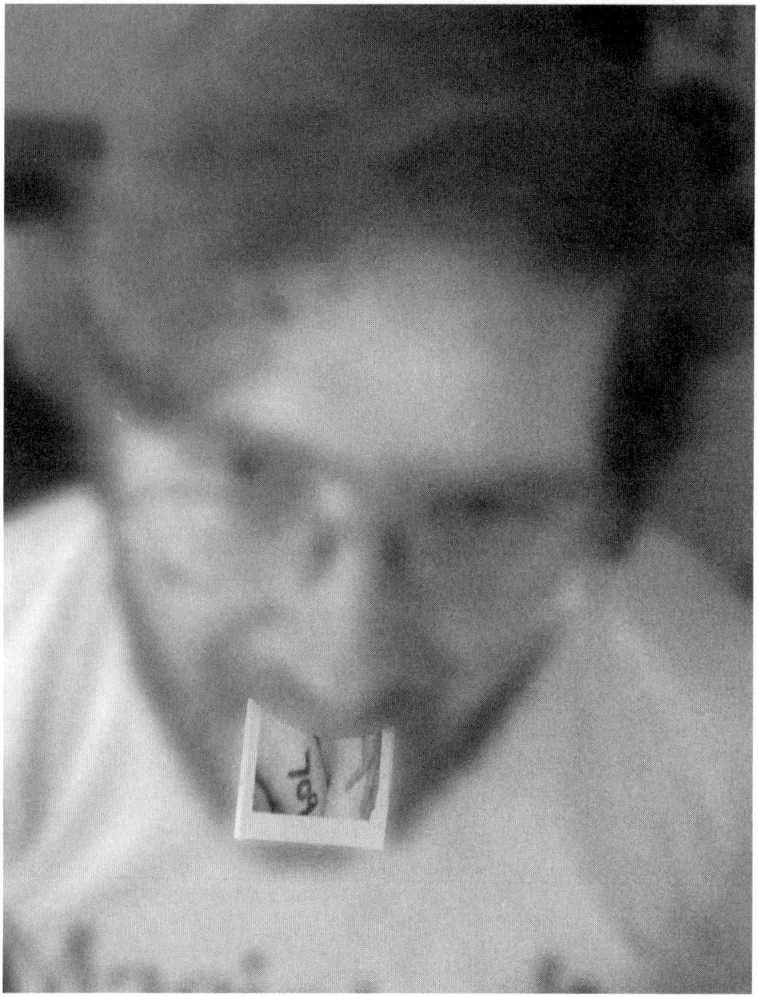

I am a connoisseur and a cunning linguist

[07/19/01 @ 10:20am]

[this poem is intentionally *tongue* in cheek]

I like to take my time
tell you tall tales
taste your lines
trace each arch

let me speak to you in tongues
and read from you in French
while I touch a nerve
here or there

scratch that, revise that to
everywhere

lie back and relax
while I take time in the telling
in twisting and turning
your mindset from sorrow to sin

I like to play with words
get creative juices flowing
with function over form
as we cum
to terms
with what
we can publish:
poetry of the pelvis

it all begins with a stroke
of my pen
across the fabric
of your fantasies

your words are
at the tip of my
tongue

how do you want me to start this story?
I only play with happy endings
like to take detours
in blending fictions with friction

I believe in long expositions
in reading you
slooow
because you are more than my muse

[I am your mouthpiece and]

you are my canvas

I'll practice on you
writing rough drafts
till I get it right
till I get it right
till you *tell* me I got it right

I am a connoisseur of your colors,
the way you coordinate your smiles
change your blues to pinks

let me paint you into smiley faces
stroke from the bottom of your canvas
up
name each smile with
whatever sound comes first

I'll use your flesh to
prove myself prolific
as I fold into
the center of your gravity

I'll write you from the inside out
and then transpose all the sounds
until they sound sexy enough
to symbolize our sin

you make me want to invent
new languages
before I exhaust your English

I am a connoisseur of your French
and the way you evoke sounds
promote poetry
provoke reactions

lie back and relax
while I try to spin you a new tale ❦

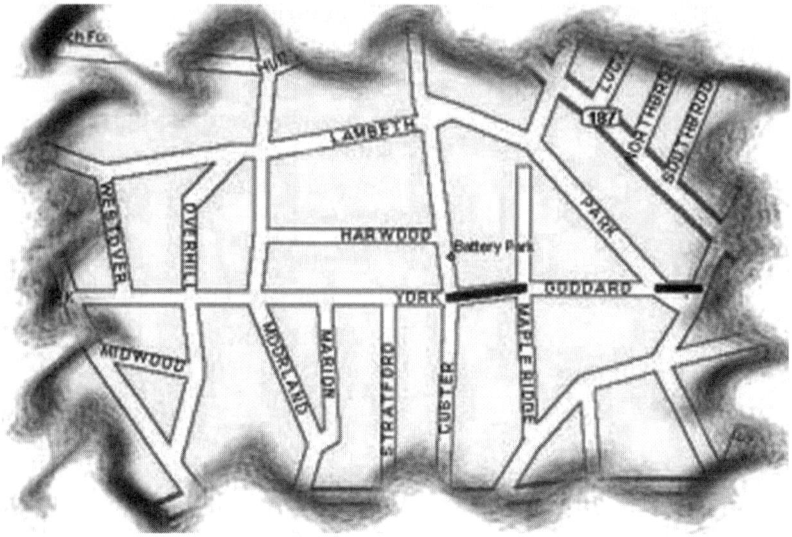

Columbia, MD... I remember

[03/28/98 @ 10:30am]

I may make a lot of this up as I go along.

The only thing I remember for sure was that it was Columbia, MD. It was 1977. I was thirteen. I was in a skating rink. And I loved her with all my heart.

Every other detail must likely be fabricated. But everything important will be absolutely true… absolutely accurate to my heart.

For the sake of argument, let's say it was every other Saturday. It could have been every other Sunday, but that's not important.

It was nine a.m. when we would leave in my step dad's blue Volvo wagon. He always liked to get an early start. And, for a weekend, I consider that *very* early.

It was a thirty-minute drive from our house in Columbia to Bethesda where we would pick up my two newly acquired stepsisters.

My real father had died when I was five… I have no memories of him. When I was thirteen my mother remarried and we moved to Columbia, MD. Within one year she would be divorced. Sometimes you realize a bit late that you really need to love… and sometimes you just can't. Within one year we would be back in White Plains, NY, exactly one block away from where we started.

But that year in Columbia, MD, is the year I will never forget. The way my heart works just won't allow it.

My step dad, Lou, had custody of his two daughters every other weekend. And these are the days I remember.

My step dad, my brother Doug and I would load ourselves into the 1974 Volvo Wagon, the deluxe model with power windows, FM radio and air conditioning. I would always sit in the rear left seat. As soon as we started to drive I would look out the window, noticing everything and paying attention to nothing. Columbia was filled with roads that were 100% planned but only 80% complete. There were supposed to be no telephone poles… all the wiring was supposed to be underground. But down the street we had a continuous strip of poles. Sometimes things don't follow their plans... they don't end up like they should.

We would get on the highway and pass a pool store. I have never been a swimmer but I always wanted an in-ground pool. This thought would distract me almost every time we made the trip.

But mostly I was thinking of Jen.

She was twelve and had long, straight blonde hair. She had a simple beauty that sometimes needed a forced smile to be noticed. When she had a true smile, she glowed. To me, when she wore that smile, on those sometimes too rare occasions, she was the most gloriously gorgeous girl I had ever seen.

When we arrived we would go inside her mother's house for a few minutes until Jen and Beth were ready, not more than two or three minutes. I never knew what to call Jen's mother, so I never used a name. She was older than my mother and not nearly as beautiful… but she was a quiet and sweet lady. I wish I had gotten to know her better that year.

Out by the car I made sure I got to the door first and held it open for Jen. Beth, the elder sister by a year, would always grab the front seat and get her own door. But I would always hold the door for Jen. My mother raised me to be a gentleman always. And my heart did motivate me to do the right thing.

Jen would sit in the middle with my brother to her right and me to her left. During the drive back I would do anything but look out the window… my attention was now inside the car.

We would all talk about school and movies and many other unimportant things.

Jen would talk about horses and animals and she would smile every time. This was the important stuff… the things that made Jen smile.

Jen and I were both victims of superior siblings; both bright but clearly not in the same league as our elder kin. She took it harder. Her smile was blocked by her falsely perceived inadequacies.

But when she would talk of her animals, then she was radiant; radiantly beautiful and bright and special.

During this year of weekends together I would fall in love with both sides of her smile: the one that radiated and the one that was absent.

After a quick lunch at Taco Bell we would drive into the corporate park in Columbia and were dropped off at Skateland. Again I would hold Jen's door.

Inside, I would sit out a few rounds as Jen, my brother, and Beth began skating.

Skating frightened me then. It still scares me now. I never knew how to stop. It always seems liked too stupid an idea to tip the feet forward and use the brakes. It seemed liked a somersault waiting to happen. Instead, to stop I would always slam myself into a wall.

I would sit out a few minutes staring at a huge painting of a jet airplane on the south wall at the narrow end of the rink… the opposite end of the snack bar.

Eventually I would start skating. Occasionally, I would catch up with Jen, Beth, or my brother and exchange a few words. They were far more accomplished skaters, so it was rare that I would catch up.

The entire purpose of these excursions was to be in the same room as Jen and most specially, most magically, to wait for the couples' dance.

The lights would dim. "*Muskrat Love*" by Captain & Tennille would start to play on the P.A.. I would find Jen, take her hand, enter the rink and we would *float*. In these laps, holding her hand, I had such grace… *we* had such grace.

Through the touch of her hand and the tears that never quite formed in my eyes I knew I was completely and absolutely in love. Never in my life have I felt so complete.

I would count each lap by noticing the airplane on the South wall each time it came around, then my attention would focus on Jen and our hands until we completed another lap. By the time the plane came around again I had forgotten my count. Love strangely effects concentration and memory… but when you are in love, skating in Skateland of Columbia, MD, holding hands with the lady you truly love and have never kissed, then who really cares about the details? Who cares how many laps, who cares if it's Saturday or Sunday or what, exactly, the song is on the P.A. system?

I was in love.

I am in love… always… with the girl who is now a woman married to another man.

I am in love with this memory.

Every lap around I would think about a first kiss with Jen that would never happen.

I still think about a first kiss with Jen that will never happen.

The song would end. The lights would come up. Wistfully, I would let go of her hand… and slam myself into a wall. ❦

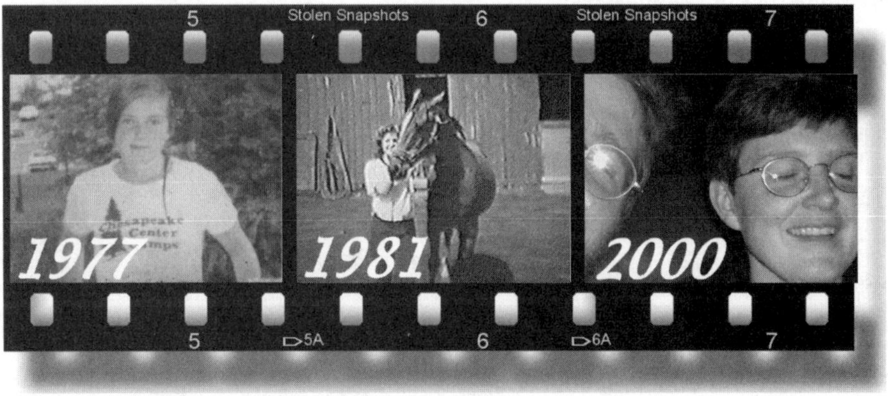

Complicating simplicity

[03/28/2000 @ 7:45pm]

Mistaking emerging emotions and
margarita motives

motivated by fear
and fearlessness

entering your early exit
something that never started

stopped

simply avoiding
avoiding heart

misplaced
misspelled
out of key
out of sync
but, still, couldn't you hum your song?
same rambling song and
tune into *more-of-som*e me

but you are busy
PLANning nothing
when there is nothing
to plan

working
forward to backward
in steps of 10 times 10

forgive me

forgive me for faking
I cared too much
...
or too little

it's all in the middle
when it SIMPLY never began

begin again simply
SIMPLY kiss me *please*
please don't forget
FORGET to remember
remember US and THEN

jump back
then step forward
forward to me
ONE step at a time

it's that SIMPLE ❦

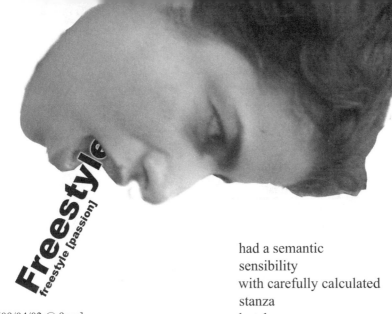

Freestyle
freestyle [passion]

[09/04/02 @ 9pm]

My girlfriend gives me shit
for writing sex

She says it's selling secrets
for smiles,
accolades and audience applause

She says it's sort of a sickness
when private parts
are made public

But I once
had a lover
who freestyled* poetry in bed

In the heat of passion
she would summon sounds
more structured than most;
a sequence of syllables
that actually made *sense* and
put a lovely language to
what we were learning about
each other

Her moans were almost always in
iambic
and her screams
had a semantic
sensibility
with carefully calculated
stanza
breaks

She was a *sensational*
writer

And, by the end of each encounter
everything would come together
in place
and be properly punctuated

My girlfriend still gives me shit
for ever saying so ❦

* "freestyle" is improvised poetry…
something done only by more talented
poets than me.

contrasting sentiment structures
[02/28/02 @ 6:00pm]

Truth be told,
I never trusted her enough
to fuck her

over the course of
2 years I only wanted to
make love

hate to say,
but, truth be told,
I never trusted her enough
to love her

still

born a believer
in love
losing becomes a pattern
I *learn* to hate

love doesn't have so much sense
as to set
criteria for caring ❦

telegram

[08/30/02 @ 1am]

need to write poem [stop]
at loss 4 words [stop]
[and] have lost all pencils [stop]
do u remember [stop]
how 2 jump start me? [stop]
remember once u
taught me some trick [stop]
involving salt, lime, liquor and lips [stop]
possibly [short] shot glass and
carefully cupped cleavage were involved [stop]
can't remember proof [stop]
of spirits [stop]
it seemed to work then [stop]
revitalized writing [stop]
lost recipe [stop]
please send self in [return] addressed
postage paid envelope [stop]
enclose sharpened # 2 [stop]
then [[stop]]
don't [stop]

corner of Syntax & Sense

[07/30/02 @ 12:00pm]

careful, crisp prose
takes me by the hand
down roads I'd never see
makes me a better poet

and there sandwiched
between the children of Omaha Beach
and a Boston bar
called "Crossroads"
I forget to say good bye
to my last lover

for a while
she has the good sense
to chuckle with
me about hole homonyms
and other such syntactical
structures

but she leaves me
in shorthand
leaving a note
of only punctuation

period. period. comma, exclamation!

it marks the end of a *very* short story

it must have been when I left
her to air dry
while I was on the road
searching for a new sound

maybe an instrument,
a fiddle, to play

when it comes to prose
the devil is always,
always
in the details

and lost in the city streets
trying to find the corner
of Syntax & Sense
I forget all about my lover

i get lost in the lush landscapes
(and sometimes the liquor)
of this place and that
and, with or without
a new poem,
I can't quite find my way home ❦

***"don't be sad"*, they say**
[10/10/2001 @ 4:42 pm]

Don't be sad, they say,
they say so seriously!

don't be sad, they say
that she went away

don't be busy waitin'
for THAT woman!
…
I can't be waitin'

no, not me, can't be

I can't be waitin'

can't do it, no can do

Instead, you see, I'm
too busy crying
to be expectin' she'll be knockin'

too busy dreamin'
to be sleepin'
thinkin' she'll be wakin' me soon

too busy wipin'
so many kisses from my lips

I am
too busy knowin'
that I am failin' so
at forgettin'
that she kissed me from the inside out
instead of the outside in

ya know, the decent way
to deceive and discard

I'm too busy countin' the seconds
to be doin' nothin' much at all

Ya see,
before she walked away,
before I was busy
bein' broken

with a ***kiss,***
I was the only one aware
of how much she *really* cared

but she was too busy walkin' away
to sit down and see how busy I was
droppin' her some tears ❦

tall poem
11/13/02

This is
my token
tall poem

slender
like I
once was
before all
the beer
binging

narrow,
broken
by too
many
line
breaks

***tall* like**
I appear
when I
do what I
do

still,
I have
to stop
here
and apologize
for running
out of
space
before I have
a chance to
say...
to say
what you
really
need to hear
me say...

ECUMENICAL BABBLING by Zork

[08/11/00 @ 10:10am]

[Please note: Elvis Mitchell is my second favorite film critic. I simply was totally perturbed I didn't know one silly word.]

RE: "'Bless the Child' is an ECUMENICAL suspense story, directed by Chuck Russell with an attempt at the hushed elegance of 'The Sixth Sense.'"
– ELVIS MITCHELL of *The New York Times* Film review [08/11/2000]

There ought to be laws and sometimes lawyers, priests and maybe punishers, to deal with this, and when, oh when, will Mr. Dennis Miller realize he may be best suited to be a *NY Times* film critic.

And who let Elvis back in the building and why is he doing film reviews anyway? I must wax on and then wax off CRITICALLY of that choice. And I could have sworn his last name was "Presley" and not "Mitchell", but then I guess it's all about being incognito when you paint prose in black & white.

But, then again, how can one be [anonymous, secreted (no such word)] incognito when starting a review with the word "ecumenical" in the first sentence.

"*Bless This Child* is an ECUMENICAL suspense story."

God, I knew it was supposed to be a [awful, ghastly, horrific, appalling] bad movie, but I never once understood it to be an inspiration for obscure adjectives.

Ecumenical, I am a poet_of_sorts and know the word doesn't have a damn rhyming scheme. It has no poetry and possibly no attainable DOCUMENTED definition. In Microsoft Word I checked through all the SCROLLS [bars].

Normally, when watching the divinely funny *Dennis Miller Live*, I am smart and savvy enough to keep my Webster's UNabridged dictionary and a thesaurus nearby for quick reference during one of his witty, heated RANTS. With GOD-speed I have learned to flip and find. But today, while driving to work listening to Van Morrison, I was sinfully lax and left the thesaurus at home next to my still unread copy of *some* Melville opus and Dante's *INFERNO*.

I read reviews during RED traffic lights and sometimes when driving behind *someone's* Aunt Martha. Please don't tell my insurance company. My premiums would get HELLish.

Today it was a review of some bad Kim Bassinger flick with even worse REVIEWS.

"ecumenical."

Being quick witted and wanting to protect and shield myself from my obviously insane ignorance of the English language I rushed to my desk at work and my copy of Microsoft Office 2000.

launched WORD.

looked for word.

"ecumenical."

I must define this word. I must know. Maybe I lost it. Maybe it was that time I went scorpion bowling at Boston University and was so nauseous I overflowed *two* sinks *and* the restaurant's toilet with regurgitated toxins.

GOD knows I burned some brain cells that night.

Maybe I lost the word then. Along with…

along with…

DAMMIT, I forget… that *other* word I forgot that night.

"ecumenical."

Frantically typing and misspelling the word I don't know in MS Word 2000.

I must know… I must REknow… I must [cash in, release, transfer, OOPPPPS] REDEEM myself, my vocabulary, my very soul, spirit and intellect.

For CHRIST'S sake, I'm a poet_of_sorts, after all.

"ECUMENICAL."
Maybe that time when I was five and my brother and his friend Danny were beating me up... back when I was SMALLER than them and suffered their [anger, rage, fury] WRATH. Maybe then. Maybe when they suffocated me for a few minutes, when I literally *and* figuratively have lost memories of brain cells gasping for air and giving themselves their very own, VERY brief eulogies. Because, while brain cells do want [tributes] eulogies, they are normally too dim and solitary to write them themselves unless in a carefully coordinated collaborative effort.

Anyhow, maybe I lost the word then.

"ECUMENICAL."
DAMN… in my frenzy I keep mistyping that word.

I am so, so [dim, thick, obtuse, dense] stupid. Soooo damn STUPID!!!!

"ECUMENICAL."
Once again… word not found… no synonyms… properly spelled. No squiggly lines under it in MS Word.

It's properly spelled, but no definition.

In MS Word 2000, not that VERY dim, dark and dank 97 or 98 version. In the *new* millennium version.

WHEW. Bill Gate's brainchild is equally dim as me. And, while he may be a trillionaire, I am not sure I can take comfort in associating myself with him in this or any other paragraph… regardless of the semantics of it all.

So here [not HEAR] I sit, still wondering "ECUMENICAL"… I know I can guess it [write, rite] right. I know, I *think* I [no] know, what it means… *almost* know what it means. Like a distant bright light I can almost FEEL it's definition… like a light at the end of a distant dichotomy.

But in the end it just leaves me wondering who let Elvis back into that *NY Times* building. The fact that he put me in such a frenzy with his review this morning makes me want to TWIST & SHOUT [capitalized just for the HELL of it!] But that is an entirely different band and they would never have written this REVIEW.

If you ask me Mr. ELVIS is a CRITIC and not a REVIEWER. And therein, within and without, meshed in the semantics of it all is the distinction of these two concepts.

CRITIC.

REVIEWER.

Bring back Plato and I know exactly which title he would put on his business card. I love the man and the mind, but I think he would think dimly of me.

R U 1 of us, or 1 of THEM?

So do be analytical and JUDICIOUS of this email.

Then define that pesky word.

And be certain to be DIVINELY CRITICAL and judicious and REVIEW all the facts. Be true to your art, your soul, or just give me your opinion.

How are you today? And what movie did you see this weekend and how did it make you *feel*?

Use your language and let it use *you*.

GOD knows that is why we are all here after all. ❦

11 step program to nowhere FAST

[06/16/01 @ 1pm & 05/30/02 @ 5pm]

I	One line at a time.
II	You smile across the room, I slip myself into the foreplay of my fantasy
III	Forget you've been broken before as I fall into your mouth
IV	Interrupting first kiss, you say, *"My God, you taste so good!"*
V	It was a Wintergreen Certs® in my mouth It must have been the Retsyn® that filled you up with reckless romance Nonetheless, I'll take the credit

VI	You dare at the doorstop to stop: *"What if you came up?"* My hand has traveled too far down for me to not go up
VII	*"Let's take this slow,"* you say. But, hot diggity damn lady, you move so *fast* We learn quickly not to listen to ourselves Luther play softly, while we play hard
VIII	We taste each other's appreciation understanding carnal chemistry get to know one another in fast forward frenzy with sensational sensations
IX	*"Hello, my name is [fill_in_the_blank]* *and I am damn glad to meet you!* *Damn glad to meet you!* *Damn glad to meet you!"* As you gasp, I say *"hello"* I already know how you are doing
X	Waking up, academic ambitions and fear of falling create cracks in the foundation of a future and our romantic rapture reveals we will separate before breakfast before boredom
XI	We kiss hello/goodbye And, feeling the heat of another *"hello,"* we take this slow just one more time Not for romance … just one for the road

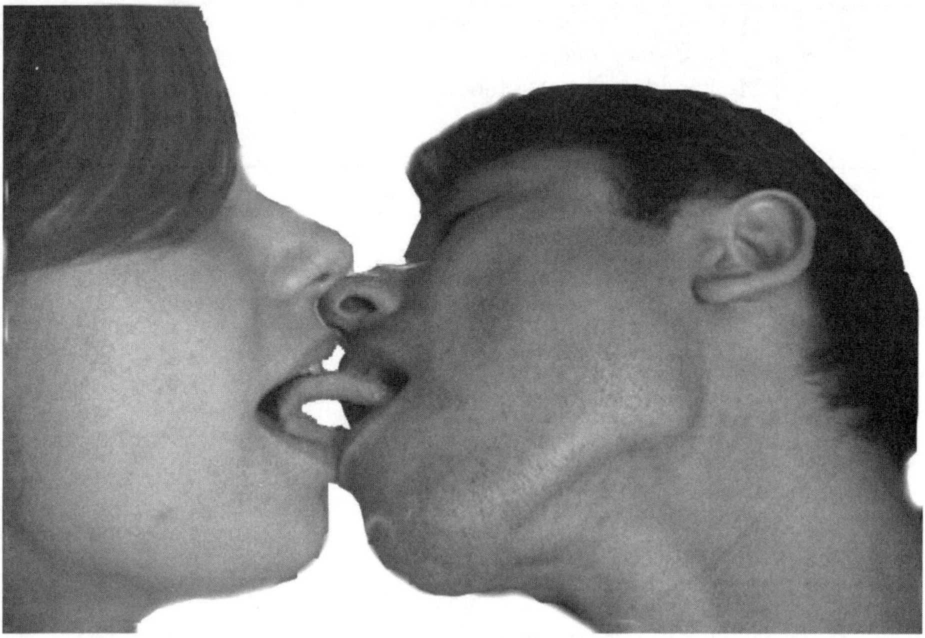

Exceeding expectations ... tasting of onion rings

[05/21/99 @ 12:47am]

Sunday night
diner parking lot
first kiss
a delicious goodnight
prolonged with a hug
prolonged with a second kiss
no a third
or was that a fourth?

Exceeding fourth kiss
expecting another

Prolonged
belonged
held and holding

Expectations
already high
exceeded

Hands caressing
too long for a goodbye
a good night

What's with this 12:20 a.m. curtain call
in this sleepy shut-down town?

Held and holding
caressing

Slowly
saying goodnight

Carefully
saying hello

Silently
deliciously
saying "till next time"

Exceeding expectations
and tasting of onion rings ❦

lost in the found

at Grand Central Station
stuck in the post partum stage
of a spectacular first kiss
I stand dumbfounded
between tracks 29 and 30

Inbound came her tongue
which stayed at this stop
for a while

But then, as all things in a depot,
there must be an outbound
[for every inbound]
so as not to overflow
the station

And now I am stuck here
between tracks at midnight,
between last and first trains,
and I have a few minutes
more to determine
if I am coming
or going ❦

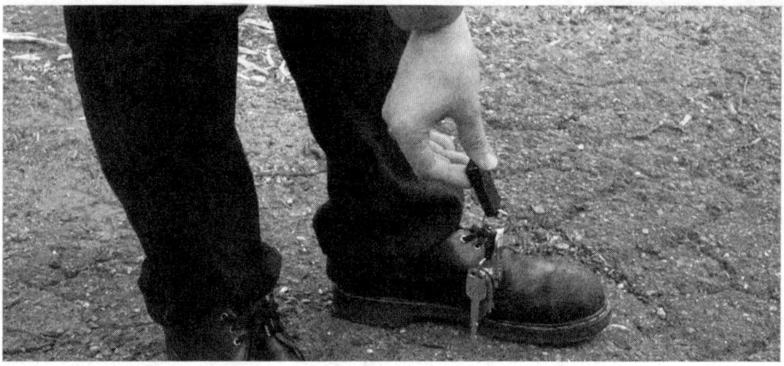

Excuse the tears [First night we didn't kiss]

[1/1/99 @ 1:40am]

Excuse the tears.

It's New Year's Eve.

On the first night I didn't kiss her goodnight there was a full moon.

She's Brazilian and was living with her aunt. After dinner on our first blind date she took me downstairs. Yes, you heard me right, she took me downstairs.

She trusted me.

There was all the normal first date awkwardness, there was no instant magic or chemistry

... this was not a magical night

... but I liked her... almost immediately, I liked her.

Remember, it's New Year's eve now... and this story has no happy ending... no happily ever after. I've written plenty of poems about this lady but we never really developed what you need for poetry.

At least not poetry that persists.

But I liked her... and after 90 minutes with her and her aunt... she asked me alone to the basement.

... where we talked... we just talked.

But it struck a sensational chord with me that she wanted to be alone with me.

I am horrible with signals, signs, astrological coalitions and all the other indicators or vibes or whatever connections are called between two people.

My shyness is epic… although you'd never guess that if you saw me standing on chairs reading poetry

… but this night was before I was standing on chairs.

So we talked… about absolutely nothing important… although I could tell you her name is not really Teka… she stole the name. But that is a story for another time.

At 11:45 p.m. I start to make a polite exit… one thing I would later learn from acting class and poetry readings is that you never want to overstay your welcome and you always want to leave them wanting more.

And, quite simply, this evening is going so well
… I'd like to end it just where it is.

I will not kiss her goodnight tonight… it's too soon… I'm too shy.

At the door I put on my coat… it is a cold October night.

I will say my good-byes in the foyer and walk to my car… I will dare the call in 48 hours to ask her on a second date… minus the aunt.

She opens the door and steps outside. This confuses me at first because she is the one that lives here and I am the one leaving.

But, being a bright guy, I figure it out… she is walking me to my car.

If I were a woman I would say to myself how gallant or sweet this gesture is. Being a man… I just hold a private smile.

She likes me.

Yes, I could say that… she actually must like me… imagine that… she's walking me to my car… in the cold… a whole 25 feet… because she likes me!

A bit dazed and delirious from a totally delightful night, I never even saw her put on her coat.

I have already said my "thank you"s and "goodnight"s in the foyer… so I don't quite know how to behave or what to say now.

So I fumble with words, fumble with my feet, and my hands, and my keys. Quiet simply I fumble.

But there is a full moon. And she is staying here with me and all my fumbling. We aren't killing time, we are protracting it… extending it… exploiting it.

To be quite honest I want to leave quickly… or else I will have to kiss her… not want to… but have to! And it is too soon for that… where I come from that's a second date thing.

She comments on the moon. What does that mean? I wonder.

It means I should kiss her… but I don't.

Instead, I fumble with the words and gestures and with the moments under this October moon.

I don't notice the cold or the clouds of visible breath we create.

I will kiss this lady soon… but not tonight.

…

On the first night I didn't kiss her there was a full moon.

Excuse the cliché: "That was then."

Tonight, I *also* didn't kiss her.

It's been 375 days since I last kissed her.

It's New Years Eve.

Excuse the tears. ❦

candlelight [burn, baby, burn]

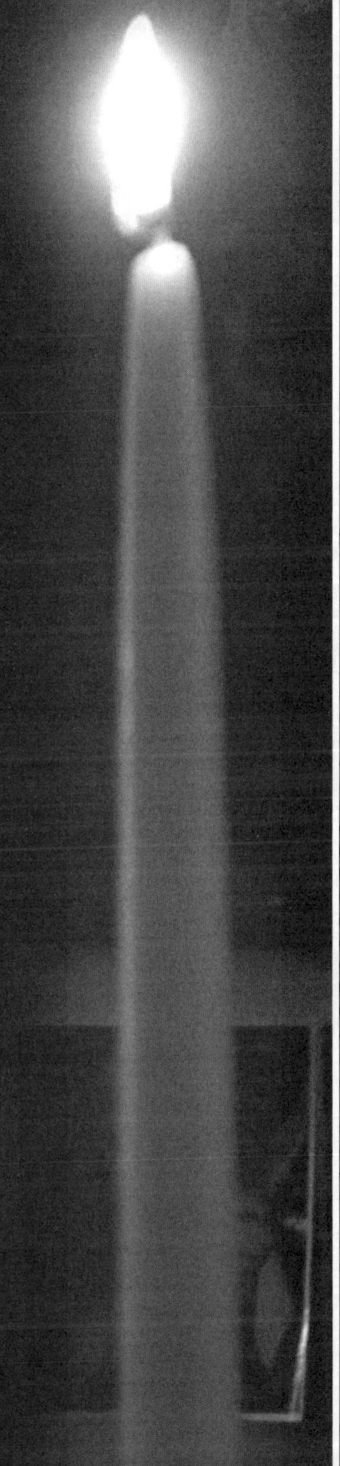

I can only write you down
by candlelight
otherwise I get you
all wrong
and make myself too clear;

it's better when
I stumble
in your dimness

I remember you best with
sepia
tones
dripping from the heat
and melting from your top
down
down
down

turning on the lights
would simply
snuff you out
fade your flame
and make me sleepless through dawn

lyrics limp till the sun sets again;

till the sun sets again, till I can
light you up again
one match, one candle at a time ❦

first person a capella

[06/21/02 @ 4:00pm]

Switched on by
horrendous need,
he turns pen to paper
or, being a gigantic geek,
keyboard to computer
and lets it
take him somewhere
he can write alone,

stash secrets
about sex, sins,
and single women

each stroke
meant to emphasize
the embarrassing
tidbits

techniques of tongue
and other such telling things
to titillate
he stashes secrets
in a silent safe
pen and paper
keyboard and computer

stashes secrets
then reads them aloud
not because he doesn't
care what someone else would say,
but being clueless is key
when girlfriends
worry he
will showcase things
best left
under wraps
and surely he will

Assuming egocentricity,
Oh, he'll tell
he'll tell
but still, they like it when he
sings to them in bed
a capella
songs without
sheet
music ❦

fourth person

[06/26/02 @ 11:45pm]

first
I was asked to
write a poem
in the fourth person

pause
prepare
pen to paper
ear to *EVERY*thing imaginable

close eyes
skip breath

reinvent beauty of that
first kiss in diner parking lot
with scent of smoke sticking to skin
taste of onions
lamp of headlights
passing by
bearing witness

stop the scene and
sense

close eyes
skip breath

and, in the Fourth,
it goes something like… ❦

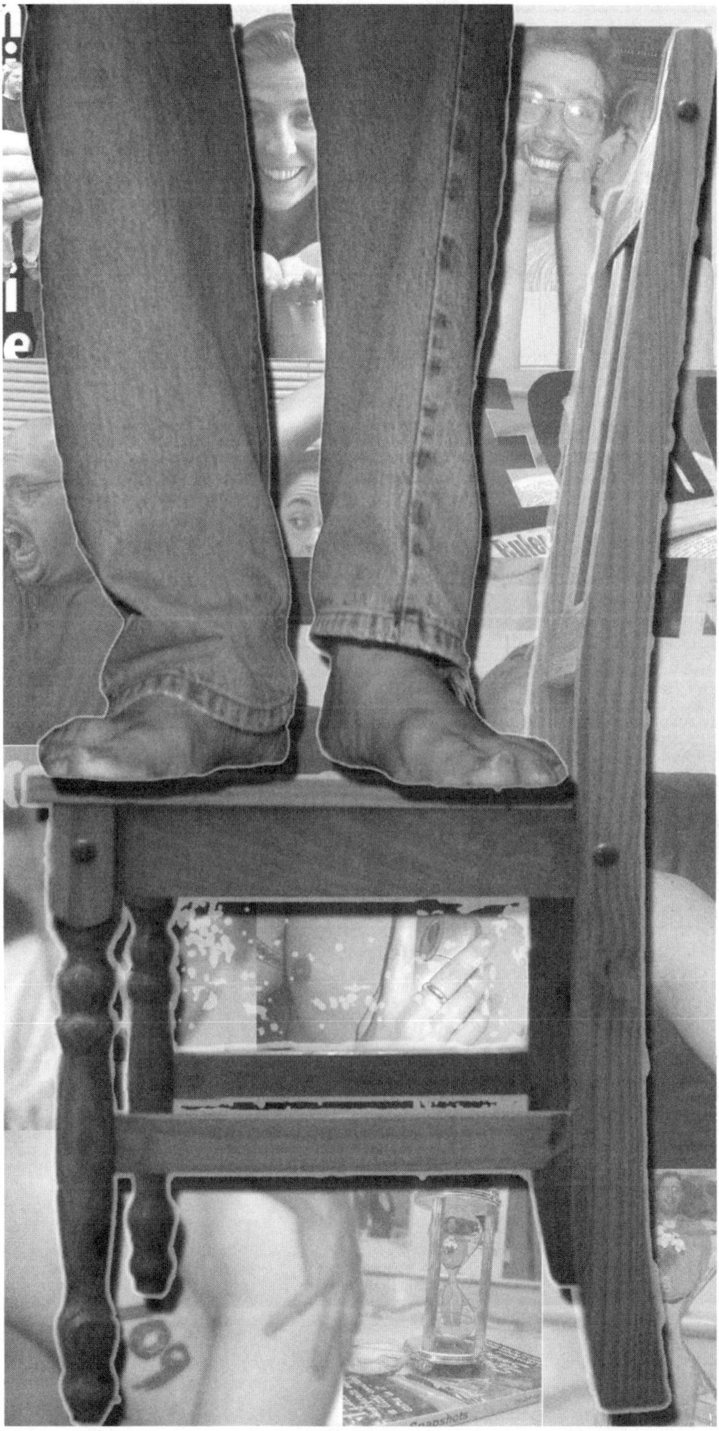

Halloween

[10/20/00 @ 9:15am]

H	Haunting hallows of Halloween
A	amazingly, always aspire agony about
L	love long lost
L	lustful longings
O	of October obituaries of
W	will, want, & wayward ways
E	even exchanging
E	even evoking, ever enchanting
N	nighttime needs, naughty necessity, & niiiice nights not [k]nown, not now, not never & nowhere near November

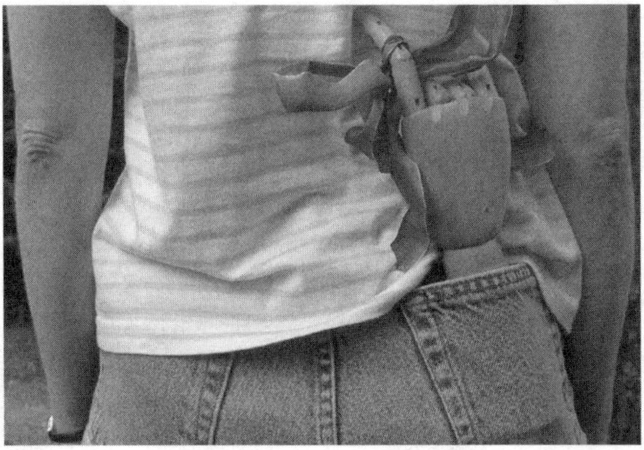

Hand please

[6/24/97 @ 12:50am**]

"Hand, please," I say as I drive her home.
She gives me her hand and everything is right.
Her touch makes it that way.
She lightly moves her finger across the back of my hand.
It's a light touch.
But the moment is anything but light.
Two bodies and two spirits connect in the simplest of ways.
This is so right!
I take my hand back to make a sharp turn on Route 9A.
When back on the straightaway I repeat, "Hand, please."
It's hardly safe while driving, a risky ritual, but well worth plenty of peril.
I feel her warmth. I feel each finger.
We have patented a finger dance of sorts
as my thumb slowly massages the back of her hand.
This woman's hand is clasped in mine and mine in hers.
I am driving her home.
In moments she will be home.
It will sadden me until I can hold her hand again.
I pull into her driveway.
The automatic light comes on.
Soon now I will lose her touch.
The car is in park now… the ignition is off.
Soon, real soon, I will let go.
For now, for a moment more, I will hold on.
It's such a simple pleasure, but so real… so important.
Please, just a moment more, let me hold her hand.
Our hands still have dancing to do as our palms continue their kiss. ❦

13

He said/she said

[03/21/01 @ 8:30pm]

When he stands in her shoes he says:
"I seek to stand alone."

When he stands in his own shoes he says:
"I need your need."

She says:
"Fierce independence fights for my solitude
my sense of self without surrender, without compromise."

He says:
"Surrender yourself to me again *and for the first time. And fight fiercely for my fancy, like you did at first."*

She says: *"First I need to find myself."*

He says: *"Find yourself in what you lost."*

She says: *"What have I lost?"*

He says:
"I have lost the beauty of your soul as it slips
under the cracks in your heart
I have lost your smile and your surrender.

I do not need to be your love... just your lover"

When together, they sit on circular benches, slide dangerously close.
Then and there they order from the same menu and sip the same wine
Then and there is when what she said IS what he said:
"Kiss me... do it now!"

Paying the check they slide apart.

She says:
"Do you ever need a change? I have dreams to discover and dances to do. I have men to meet and first kisses to covet."

He says:
"Don't you remember meeting me and coveting our kiss?"

She says:
"I don't dare rob myself of romances yet undiscovered."

He says:
"Don't you remember discovering me?*"*

She says:
"What if I can do better? What if new would be nicer? What if an amorous answer could stop my questioning? What if I can finally *find fulfillment?"*

He says:
"Till when again? Your distraction robs me of our romantic recollections. Your kiss was the second very best."

She says:
"I am not yet satisfied. I cannot sit still and settle."

He says:
"Settle down.
Forgive me for forgetting to forget you
and being careless enough to care constantly."

She says:
"I weigh emotions in drink and throw darts at frightening feelings. I paste them to bar walls and these walls are made of brick and mortified fears of surrendering my solitude."

He says:
"I never came, but she surely went."

She says:
"Come on now, really, I never really came
over into your heart."

He says:
"Tonight, touch me tenderly from your insides out & tell me a fable of satisfying sweetness & forgetting fears."

She says:
"Your constant caring crowds me. My tomorrows terrify me... even today."

Even after orgasms their dialogues divert, even when left unsaid.

When in bed, he speaks silently with digital dexterities and teases with an unspoken tongue until ***she says:***
"Don't stop... I'm cumming."

Yet, she stops… coming into his life
stops seeing and seeking the shelter of his soul and the rapture
found within his hold.

He says:
"Don't stop... seeing & seeking me... simply understand the simplicity of staying."

Who decides which side to find truth in when what she says never has the heart, home and hold of what he says and when what he says never has the wisdom to stop caring that she ever said *"don't stop"* at all? ❦

I got PHIL tea

not coffee

he likes tea

On the 4th day

LILI & I

bonded

I got drunk

with

Baryshnikov

... i have a photo

Hello, my name is Zork

[10/02/98 @ 9:01am]

"Hello, my name is Zork."
I am the world's most romantic man… but this is not about that.
This piece is all about name dropping.
You know I worked with PHIL Collins… twice.
I covered my body with name tags saying *"Hello, my name is Zork."*
"I'm Zork and you're not!"
"Zork, it's not just a name… it's a way of life!"
I introduced myself and shook his hand so many times he couldn't help but remember me when we worked together three months later.

I got Phil Collins tea… not coffee… he likes tea… milk for the British… we don't understand that.

I have a photo to prove that. Do you want to see it?

"Hello, my name is Zork."
This is all about name dropping.
I worked with LILI Taylor… before she shot Andy Warhol… before she was Academy league.

She thought I was a bit odd… it might have something to do with the Viking hat and the skirt.
Don't ask… it's a longer story than you want to hear.
But on the fourth day we bonded… LILI and I.
This was after she could "*Say anything*"… and sometimes she did… sometimes she didn't.
But Joe still lies. With his eyes, he *still* lies!

"Hello, my name is Zork."
This is all about name dropping.
JOAN Cusack, I worked with her.
She could '*say anything*' but she rarely said a word.

I wonder if she saw my signs… my name tags. I don't think I amused her much.

This is about being extraordinarily ordinary.
It's about being in arms reach.

This is about rising above… through names.

PETER & Peter

Tyson, SPAWN, White?

Zork & CARLY

GINA showed me none of it

I got drunk with BARYSHNIKOV and loaned my computer… no my MACINTOSH… to PETER Gallagher.

A spectacular SPAWN, played by Michael J. White [ironically a big black man] beat me up with a *loaf of bread*. But my FRIEND'S friend is KILLER CLOWN, a gooey sort of green guy played by that Latin legend LEGUIZAMO.
Spawn will pay… he'll pay!

"Hello, my Name is Zork."
I worked with STEVE Buscemi… before he was diced in a Fargo wood chipper… before Armageddon came and went.
Before he lamented being PINK… Mr. Pink.

He doesn't remember me… someone asked him… but I have the photo to prove it.
Do you want to see?

"Hello, My name is Zork."
This piece is all about name dropping
… about standing out.
I'm 6'5" and a half … I used to be short
… willpower.

Hannibal Lecter's dear, dear friend TOM Noonan has called *ME* short… but here I stand, standing tall… just a bit terrified, but tall none-the-less.

RON Jeremy taught me a trick or two of his trade for foreplay with fine femmes.

Ron's blurb for my book is *cumming soon*… you might want to stand out of the way!

JOE BOB Briggs blurbed my book. He mentioned Mimi's mammaries as motivation.

CARLY Simon, STILLER & MEARA, GILBERT Gottfried… even the Night Stalker have suffered striking an all-too patient pose for the purpose of celluloid stamina with *me*.

SOUPY threw pie

GILBERT liked me ...I have a photo

STEPHEN is scary but GREAT and STILL not in poem!

I have photos, do you want to see?

GINA Gershon showed me none of it before she was BOUND as a SHOWGIRL.

I worked with them all. I'll drop their names… to get your attention.

I had SOUPY Sales throw a pie in my face.
I thought it was funny. I don't know if he agreed.
But I have a photo… do you want to see?

Paul Shaffer shared a snapshot
securing *his* place in *my* picture portfolio.
Do you want to see?

This is about me wanting to be you… be with you...
dreaming you would want to be me… with me.

I stand on chairs… to be taller.

I'm the world's shyest guy, but I speak louder.

"Hello, My name is Zork."

Will you remember me?
Will you tell your friends… *"Hello, HIS name is Zork?"*

This piece is about being noticed, being remembered, and getting your attention.

Do I have yours?

Will *you* be my friend?

Will you date me? Will you kiss me and hold me real tight?

Do you think I am sexy?

Does it have anything to do with PHIL or CARLY?

"Hello, my name is Zork."
I have five words in a feature film… a TROMA film… do you want to hear them?

STEVE forgot me [imagine that!?]

RON knows a trick or 2

LEGUIZAMO's friend!

"Hello, my name is Zork."

Will you remember me!? Will you drop *my* name!?

Will you honor me!? Will you keep me close to your heart and mind and never let me go!?

What's my name?

What is my name!?

WHAT IS MY NAME!!!??

...

[quietly... calmly]
"Hello, my name is Zork."

What's yours? ❦

Her head lies resting on my chest

[6/13/97 @ 5:20pm]

Her head lies resting on my chest.
"I love being here with you like this," she whispers.

It's a magical collection of moments lasting well over an hour.

These are moments so simple.

There is no conversation to speak of;
there is no dance,
no sex.

There is no music in the background; nothing special about the ambience.

We are simply sitting on the couch in her living room.

"This feels so good," she whispers after a long stretch of silence.

My arm is wrapped around her. My hand is making small massaging circles across her back.

I can feel the contours of her body through her blouse.

I notice the ridge of her belt as my fingertips reach just millimeters below it.

I feel the strap of her bra as I cross over it
and the softness of her flesh that is right below the fabric.

My fingers move with the most delicate of motions and the softest of touches.

My entire attention is on the sensation under my fingertips,
the scent of her skin,
the sound of her breath,
and her occasional whisper.

A clock behind us that makes a steady tick.

I can't see it but I imagine it to be a grandfather clock.

She comments on the occasional rumble of our stomachs.

She notices each passing train in the distance.

Well over an hour her head is resting on my chest.

I would have been happy to spend years just like this.

There was nothing sexual about these moments but *everything* sensual.

This is all so simple, it's *almost* better than sex.

I can't tell you if I love this woman, or if I ever will. We barely know each other.

But there is something special in these moments we share.

Maybe they will last minutes, weeks, or even years.

I am only concerned with these moments.

They are enough for me and I hope they last as long as they can.

For tonight I have created a home for this special lady in my arms.

"I can hear the beating of your heart," she says.

She notices its rhythm.

She has been on the verge of sleep for most of this time.

She fills me with desire
… to spend more time with her. ❦

how to: write a poem

[07/12/02 @ 12:25pm]

first
separate a piece
of crisp clean paper
from stack

anything *or nothing*
can appear now

sharpen your pen
scratch that last word
edit "pen" to "pencil"

sharpen

sit, suffer
under desk lamp
search for words
wit, or *any* reason to write

possibilities can perplex when
purpose isn't plain
and pain isn't the purpose
behind pencil

sharpen pencil again
just to be sure
you start out right

sit and suffer
in sequential bursts of silence
missing inspiration in
every single, God forsaken, breath

getting bored
looking at white on white
go to fridge and find
leftovers left over
from late, late session
last night

add whipped cream
to whatever food you find;
it can even help the roast beef

gorge yourself,
it surely won't help your process,
but you were hungry about now
anyway

bloated
go back to white on white

sharpen
because it makes you feel more
purposeful and productive

carefully draw a short,
straight line

smile

the possibilities are
almost endless

success is pending;
critical acclaim and
celebrity are certain

seriously study
short straight line

will it be the top of "T"
or a sideways "I"
making you change orientation
and context

sit, suffer
under desk lamp
search for words

is it time for TV?
yeah, *that's* it,
Seinfeld surely
will sedate
and stimulate
something *or nothing*

in thirty more minutes
stay seated and surf

beer from fridge
may liberate
an idea *or not*

drift to sleep with
mustard from roast beef
sandwich on unwashed t-shirt

tonight,
again,
you *still* will certainly suck

white quilt over couch
has tucked you in
for another night
of nothing special

beer can slips to spill on shag

broadcast hours ending
snow falls from TV

white on white

TV tone forms
long straight sound

dream of flipping to page 69
November *New Yorker*
"By Line" by you

dream of poems starting with "T" tops
or sideways "I"s ❦

stolen snapshots series presents:
HOW TO:
50% off
for the
super skinny
EXTRA STRENGTH
LAXATIVE
• Nu Yuk Times Bestseller
• Over 10 trillion in print
• Foreword by Dr. U.P. Chuk
BINGING FOR
BULIMICS

how to: publish poetry

[07/17/02 @ 9:25pm]

first

don't

Poynter* points out
it is incredibly impractical
to publish poetry

how can one promote
what surely won't sell
when social sensibilities
certainly suck

so, for a poem called
"*how to: publish poetry*"

I must keep it short
and say first

don't

instead write a "how to" book
on how to *not* write
a book of poetry
how to entirely eradicate via electric shock stimulation
every such
trip of the tongue
and every inane iambic initiative

spend time pondering
how to harvest, then hide,
all your hormones
firmly flushing all your fantasies
of expressing yourself

when in social circles
silence is sometimes the best
syntax instead of saying you write
with structure, style
and carefully counted syllables

how to publish a book of poetry?

don't

maybe a book
on "*plumbing for prim and proper people*"

better than poetry and
far more practical
to play with people's pipes
when polished, practiced and/or prophetic prose
doesn't pay shit

maybe write a
how to book for bulimics

binging being an overlooked
and oft neglected art
and sometimes the end results

are even more savory
than the words and wit
you might
expel on an empty spirit

when considering writing
a series of sonnets
maybe write a book called:
math for morons

it will add up to something more
sensible than
your urge to soul search and
your other more esoteric endeavors aiming
to be overlooked
and underappreciated
by the paying public

instead,
maybe a book on *Things to do with Beer Bottles*

or *Safety with Styrofoam: the guide to non biodegradable, but heat keeping, Dunkin Donuts coffee cups*

to arrive on Amazon
try to write these:

• *How to Surf: Controlling your Controls for Couch Potatoes*

• *Chocolate Confections and confessions of such things from dead diabetics [otherwise called "How to* DIE-*a-betic"]*
or
• *Dastardly deeds for delinquents to do [or how to tick off your parole officer]*
try
• *How to cheat on your wife on $50 a day and 50 ways to clean lipstick from a horrible husband's collar*

When considering publishing a book of poetry,

don't

instead write *how to get rich books*
(otherwise known as the "*selling to sorry saps series*")

write a :
How to get rich writing 'how to get rich' books book
or a
How to get rich writing 'how to publish books on publishing'

or a *how to* book
on writing *how to* books

when pontificating
on publishing poetry
it is more economical to
shut up and commit
your purpose to perishing

Surely, Poynter will blurb your back.**

[When it comes to publishing poetry,
don't] ❦

* *Dan Poynter publishes the definitive book on self publishing, This book could not have been published without his wise words. And, if I had any sense, I would have taken his advice and not printed 10,000 copies of performance poetry.*
** check back of book, hopefully Poynter left a blurb

I am certainly a sorry sucker when it comes to Sandy

[08/24/2000]

Marci, Mimi, Mary, Martha, Molly, Megan, MAURA
maybe MAURA manipulated me… or let us call her SANDY

Sundays, because she won't surrender Saturdays, we seductively sip
extraordinarily expensive champagne
Drop drips, tongue tastes, eyes open, pulse pounds

silent sip…
… amazingly aware
… seduction

decadent deception dovetails via daylight drink and dance till dawn
don't tell Daniel
or let us call him SAM
[don't dare]

fingers slide down her side, sensual strokes stimulate, tongue teases and tastes,
suckling that sweet
soon to be sour part of her neck
… where her cunning lingers

she slurps oyster from my shell and I suck and suckle her sexy naked fingers

It is all she still offers

suffering selfishness she…

slow and sad is her suspended surrender

careless on credit cards, credentials and cadence

simply scammed

kant kiss

dark doorstep, front foyer, kareless keys kovert… found
… flawing romantic rhythm

she starts to turn cheek, checking this or that,
interrupting instinctive intimate initiative

But darling Daniel gets to dance in the dark, naked and on Saturdays

[So sorry, SAM]

Tonight, she is overdressed and I am underwhelmed, confounded and confused
by a memory of her when she served herself to me sunny side up

Short, short-lived and only sometimes sexy

Seams of her short segue slipped by me
brushing by bulge, but broken at her "seems"

Sam, solely satisfied, sleeps seconds after short spent orgasm,
Sandy sort of suffocating under his now slumbering self ❦

"I am so lucky... so blessed"

[04/04/01 @ 6:58am]

After acting annoyed in acting class
she pauses, calms, says:
"I am so lucky... so blessed"
to step inside these walls, inside my heart

An ordinary life turned extraordinary
within these four walls
and your two arms
within the repetition exercise of this smile
this mantra materializes
"I am so lucky... so blessed"

"I am so blessed with a beautiful beginning
and I am beginning to believe
in myself,
in these walls,
in your arms"

Moments later in a bar,
illuminated by the lamp
she likes like a lover, she says:
"I am so lucky... so blessed"
to step inside your smile
so blessed to sip this beer,

so happy to find my way home with
you tonight,
so lucky to begin
breaking down these walls
outside my fears
brick by brick

Take me home
dear lord,
dear lover,
please take me home
and, in bed, prove me lucky

Hours later
arm numbed as you sleep
enveloped in the pillow I am for you
awake for hours
or more
I look at you.
You wake and we find each other's
silent smile,
it's a place we linger
for hours
or more

I think, *"I am so lucky... so blessed"*

Later, as we reinvent tenderness
in touch,
in a moment of passionate rapture
we collapse, out of breath
I say, *"I am so lucky
to offer you my breath in this extended
kiss"*

For tonight,
let us be lucky to have found
a companion
with no thoughts of tomorrows

Just the same, you know I will be here

Tenderly, you touch my cheek,
tonight,
for now,
in this sexy scene,
and in this bed we bathe in,
in one rapturous night of passion,
looking only for one more
we both say,
we repeat,
we caress,
we come
together,
we come together
and say
"I am so lucky... so blessed"

Let this be our mutual monologue
tonight
our decadent dialog
our home and our hope
that we stay so lucky

Tonight,
let me remember
in your arms,
for just one more repetition,
please let me remember,
"*We* are so lucky… so blessed"
❦

That'll Do

[07/18/2000 @ 2am]

I don't have the language to stop her tears

I can't cry her a poem
to fresh mint moments and memories

diving into a sea of words
drowning in a syntax of sorrow
simply suffocating
inventing words
I can't say during her sleepless night

Instead,
I am silent
I don't have the language
to silence my fears; her tears

simplified through a process of pain

a sappy soundtrack sticks to suffering

and *"that'll have to do, babe"*
in a world of pointless pain
it'll have to do. ❦

I Dare You

[02/22/98 @ 8:00pm**]

I dare you
to let me hold you,
accept a tender touch,
and plant a careful kiss

welcome what you fear
you may cherish
and trust me totally today
(even if not tomorrow)

let your instincts initiate
everything

forget yesterday
it left you cold
and confused

forget tomorrow
it's too soon to tell
[and, stupid as it may sound,
time will tell]

drop your guard,
offer your lips,
trust my touch,
enter my arms

For ninety minutes,
I dare you. ❦

I desperately want to kiss you

[02/07/99 @ 7pmish]

You said, *"I desperately want to kiss you"*
… to *him* you said

I say, *"I desperately want to kiss you"*
No… I think…
unsaid…
unsaid…
overthought…

You eat your chili
… spoon to mouth
… and I think… I desperately want to kiss you

A congratulatory pat on the back
… and I think… I desperately want to kiss you

An overdue photographed hug
… and I think… I desperately want to kiss you

We talk and talk
and I say everything but what I think
… everything but what you said you said to someone new

What's it been? 493 unkissed days or such
… since you thought
… since we did
… think about kisses

Can't you see we have taller kisses?
… can't you see our kisses have more poetry?
… can't your lips see mine?
… want mine
… again?

As I sneak innocent gentle touches with naughty thoughts, I think
… sweet and sensitive
… patiently passionate
… warm and wild with wanting
… I desperately want to kiss you

Lady,
… can't you say?
… won't you say?
… pretty please to say
… *to me*
"I desperately want to kiss you" ❦

I will never be Billy Collins*

[08/19/02 @ 12:00pm]

Firstly, because he is famous

He has a way with words

He can captivate a crowd
[*completely]*

I had plans
to stand in stadiums
pontificating
about my pleasures and pains
and observations so keen
I cut myself on the edges
[of my stanzas]

I am not Billy Collins
and won't ever have his way
with words

When I try to keep things simple
I keep tripping all over
my tangents

My words never quite meet up the way
his do

And all of these technicalities of talent
kind of screw up my plans
to get on MTV, ABC, HBO

Any acronym that will
get me in the local papers
scratch that,
I need to be thinking bigger,
get me in *The New York Times*

Maybe in a poetry publication
where my newfound peers will
need stepladders for their syntax
to step up to my plate
and pitch prose with me

I need to be properly prioritized in
print
and the press

Something I can take
home to mom and say,
"Can't you see
I really do have something to say!"

Not that my mom doesn't
listen to me,
believe in me,
and leave me leftovers

But it seems I want
so much more
than she has to offer

More than my lover leaves me with
at the end of the night

More than your applause, nice as you
may be, can ever do for me

I need to be *famous*!

Firmly entrenched in the subconscious
of all of America's youths

I need to be bicoastal
and be thought about
by total strangers
in 3 different times zones

Simultaneously!

I want to be incredible
instantly,
totally talented,
have sex with starlets,
sing the *Star Spangled Banner*
at the Super Bowl
and sell my soul

to *matter* somehow

matter *more*

matter more than me… ❦

* Billy Collins is the Poet Laureate of the United States, and thus far more talented and famous than Zork

the real deal about being Billy

[11/19/02 @ 11:30am]

I want to make you extraordinarily ordinary

I want to use small type to print this poem to make you read
harder

I want to stand on chairs;
make you taller
from willpower alone

I want to teach you to
testify to
the power of
your broken silences

I want to preach the power of Pez
and help you practice PopTart poetry
and surge you all
with small sugar rushes
that rush straight to your lips
[and out through your loving
attention to your new-found language]

I want to throw you parties
where the pitchers are filled
with words
[I want to put them to bad music
and dance with you all to dawn]

I want to make and break
all of your hearts so
you can write me tear stained
poems

I want to make you all
wacky and weird
enough to understand
and memorize most of this poem
(except for the parts you already agree with)

I want to make *you* [*all*] poets!
[sidebar: see OpenMic next page]

So I do want to be Billy Collins:
only bigger, better
and louder ❦

PS. much love to Billy Collins. He *IS* making many more poets
[pay attention to his focus on school systems and their sensibilities]

Open MIC

Colette D'Antona

Actress

Age: 25

Poems written / published: hundreds / 0

First Poem: age 10

Poem subject: (sigh) love

Why I write poetry: Not writing poetry would be a colorless and lonely ride.

CAMELOT

A lie is worth a thousand truths
If what you're saying seeks no self
If it manages to quiet the past
Or offer comfort where none is felt

The extension of a familiar hand
Or a tiny, gently placed grin
Can heal the most weary of hearts
And fix it so measures of light can break in

How sad it is to feel hope ebbing
And belief in chance slowly slipping away
Nobody counts on the dreamer settling
Nobody bargains on regretting the day

Tell me the disillusion will be fading
That the disappointment will make me strong
Tell me pain will make me pretty
And there is no real harm in being wrong

I promise to believe what you say
I'll enchase every spoken word
Because faith is the one thing I haven't lost
And never completely could

Hope springs eternal
In countless, silly young souls
There's a lot to be said for feeling young
And in feeling silly, I'll suppose

A lie is worth a thousand truths
Tell me, good sir, what is it you see?
Take your time, precision isn't a crime
But would you mind lying to me? ❦

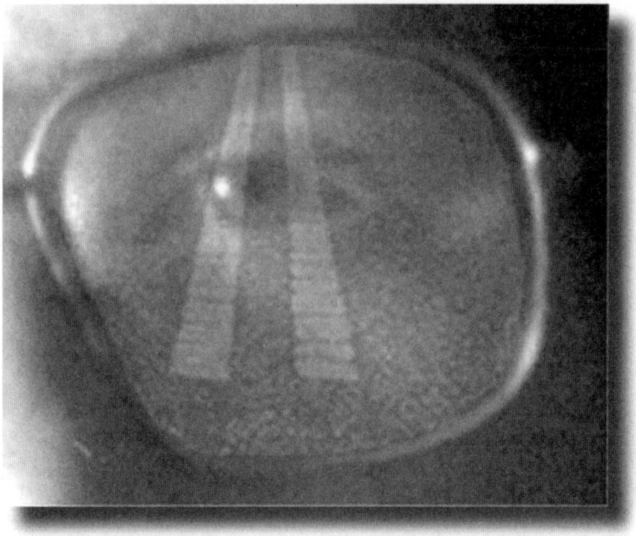

if I see you again

[01/19/03]

what will I do with my hands
when they only know how
to feel you?

Cuff them behind my back
hoping they don't notice
you're only one turn away?

If I see again
what will I do with
my eyes?

Do I peel myself an onion
and tear myself up
in avoidance of your look?

If I see you again
what will I do
with my ears to block
your vibrations
and your vocabulary
of stunningly sharp
silences?

Do I stand
in the nearest corner
turn flush to the wall
and pound my head hard
hoping all I can hear is the
numbing sound
of my forehead to hardwood?

forehead to hardwood!

And then what would I say
to put some balance back into the room
but "nah, nah, nah, nah, nah?"

And what a sight
this will be
this all will be
if I see you again
hands cuffed behind my back
banging head against the wall

What a sight to see
to see the man
still too afraid to say
"I love you"
loud enough
to start again
full of all this
numbingly beautiful
nothing
we had found ❦

This is the poem

that will NOT win
the slam tonight

You might want to take
notes [and learn from this
loser]

It's too short for you
to take too seriously
and seriously speaking
it's full of fluff

This is the poem that
will lose the slam tonight
it's too bad to memorize
and I have no friends
in the house
to act all *freaky*
when I read it

You can all feel free
to go take a leak
or go get a beer
I could use a Budweiser
if you are feeling
full of benevolence
and buying

Take your time
you have 3 minutes
because this is the poem that
will lose the slam tonight.

I didn't screw any of the
judges
and I didn't *screw*
any of the judges
so that all kind of screws
my chances
of using sex or sin to secure
a stunning
score here

I'm not mad much tonight
I've avoided all anger this
evening
I'm not angry with Agard
I'm not mad at
Marty McConnell

And I didn't even have the
sense to
write a poem about the
sizzling sex appeal
of these pin-up poets

But, as to what women want,
I know they would rather
have Roger
[get the Gold and secure the
scores tonight]

This is the poem that
will lose the slam tonight

My art was never
impoverished
and I was entirely
overeducated

I slept through
summer school
in Scarsdale

And I buy a new palm pilot
each month

This poem has no specific
structure
and is not even
sappy or sentimental

I was not molested
this month

I did not just get broken
by some big breasted
beautiful babe

My girlfriend did not
just find a better poem
to sleep with
and my penis was not put
through one of those pure
machines
by someone pissed off
with something I said or d
to someone, somewhere,
sometime

And it's been 38 years since
I got out of rehab
although every once
in a while
I do feel I need a hit of some
of that
fetal fluid for a quick fix

Maybe I'll be back
sometime soon
with *something*
to scream
about

So, this is the poem that will
lose the slam tonight

I might as well stop it
right
here!

line #9, Steven [6 from 10]

[04/06/02 @ 11:45am]

Larry, new to the place,
an unexpected element
of merger madness,
an aging alcoholic,
a golfing gentleman
and friend to someone
in the firm,
tries to add through subtraction

Not knowing the mechanics
or methods
and spared the burden of experience
and knowing better
only reads reds from blacks

He strikes through line #9
that could be read as a name,
but not now

He strikes through line #9,
not knowing impact,
unconcerned with flesh
that fed the functions of the firm
for 10 plus years;
later counted as six,
to simplify severance

Larry passes crossed out sheet
to Charles, company comptroller,
a master of math
manipulations,
sometimes sloppy with
decimals and details

In terms of severance
Charles figures 6 from 10
by seducing spreadsheets
and playing with payroll principles
to suit the color scheme
of his black and whites

In reporting to Robert Sr.,
Charles is only concerned in changing the colors
of the sheets

Make it all monochrome
forsake & forget
the history and heroes
that came before

Line #9 had
spent years squeezing 70
into work weeks
slept on couches;
built rather than burned

Fueled by caffeine and a
care for computers
he worked
as an additive rather than
subtractive
system

They forsake those who
built the bridges that they now burn
so easily

When big becomes small
& basic math loses its geometry
history and line #9 are paid no heed and severed swiftly; not sweetly

Local legend leaves no legacy,
line #9,
Steven,
married for 6
with one on the way,
is let go ❦

I have no issues

[02/10/99 @ 9am]

I have no issues
no cause… no point
I have nothing important to say
no universal lesson
nothing to preach

I have no issues but what's in my heart
but what's NOT in my arms
my issues, as my arms, are empty
my passion is pointless
it needs someone to wrap around

I have no issues but fulfilling
my selfish dream to keep you warm
whoever you are

I have no issues but to touch you,
no intent but to reach out and hold you
no vision but to find you out

I don't bother caring about the ozone layer
... not yet
... I am distracted
... by you
... whoever you are

God knows, there are issues of race & prejudice,
tolerance & understanding,
taxation & theology

but I won't preach
I can't preach
about them
not yet
till I hold you
whoever you are

I am distracted by you
... and your smile
... and our hold
... and the like that could grow to teach me about love
... again, teach me about love

I am distracted by you
... and your absence
... your anonymity

I have an issue
I have *one* issue
... to find you out
... and bring you into *our* heart and *our* hold

... wherever you are... whoever you are

you are my issue ❦

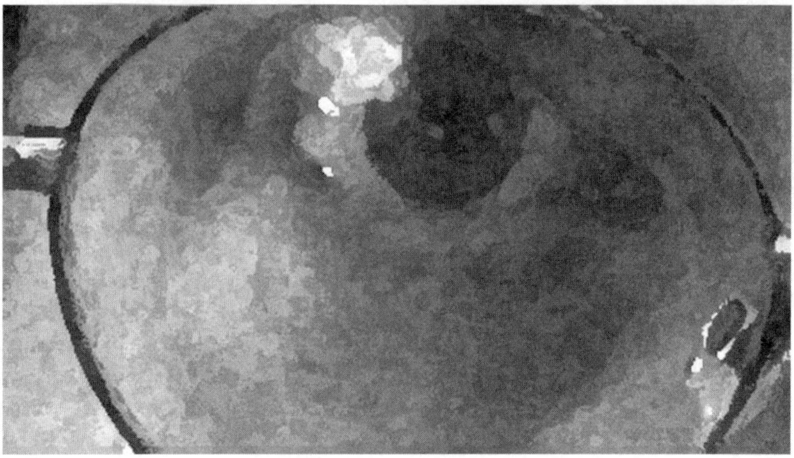

I have no mouth and I must scream.

[06/24/97 @ 6:27pm]

"I have no mouth and I must scream."

It's a Harlen Ellison story.

And it's a metaphor. I stole it from Harlen.

I have no mouth and I must scream.

I must scream to be heard.

Can you hear me?

I read at poetry readings and I write things like this.

Here are some tricks.

There must be the chorus, the repetition to be remembered.

Then the pretension. It might be rich, it might be publishable

… the false modesty to pretend that it doesn't matter… it's not worthy

… the arrogance that they might give a damn… should give a damn.

The writer sadly suffers the delusion that they can actually write.

I have no grace, I have no style, I have no nuance.

I have no mouth and I must scream.

"Don't tell me... show me... paint me a picture with words."

… some clouds, mountains, water falls, moons… nature stuff. Ebbs and Flows… They're always good.

There is the one about my heart and soul being buried under the snow,

the promise that when the seasons change my seed will bloom.

You know what I'm talking about. You've heard the song.

I have no mouth and I must scream.

There went my stolen metaphor… and my chorus.

AHHHHHHHHH!!!!!

I am screaming!!!! Can you hear me?

Such loneliness… no metaphor… just loneliness.

I have a heart of holed up haunts that needs to love; be loved.

Arms that needs to hold… and hold tight.

Lips that need to practice kissing. Can you taste my lips?

I'd like to taste yours.

Stories… to tell and to *hear*.

I need a spirit to join. A hold to share.
A *peace*… a *piece* of something called "us."

I am screaming… can you hear me?

And I think I am the only one… that needs your hold… that deserves your hold.

In acting class, semester after semester, I stand on chairs and I read these things.

And they do listen… and I am heard.

But I am in *acting* class…

Are they acting? Am *I* acting?

And maybe I am doing it to pick up the chicks

… time to think up a better strategy
… do you have any?

I read at poetry readings… can you believe that? And sometimes they listen.

Why is that?

I write about kisses. Will you kiss me?

Will you let me write about you?

I need to hold you… or is it you?

I am screaming… can you hear me?

I don't write poetry… I can't write poetry.

But I am screaming
… can you hear me?

This is what I do… and it isn't a poem… it's a scream.

I said, *"Can you hear me?!"* ❦

competing with Clinton

10/31/02 @ 1pm

There is this kid
called Clinton
who never seems to
have to search for
things to say

I see him at poetry readings
and at 17 he seems
so much smarter than me

A white boy with a
rapper's rhythm
who performs
too perfectly
for someone still
so new

I bet he gets all
the girls
and, in those awkward
courting situations,
I am sure he never
slips his syntax
and is at a shortage
of the right things to say

I've got girls with poetry too,
but at twice his age,
it took me twice
the time

And my girlfriend
often gives me shit
for the things I say
but still I say them
even though I have to wait till
she walks away

I wish I became a
poet at 17
or, better yet,
I wish I had been
born one

I might have become
so much more

Or, at the very least,
I would have become
myself sooner ❦

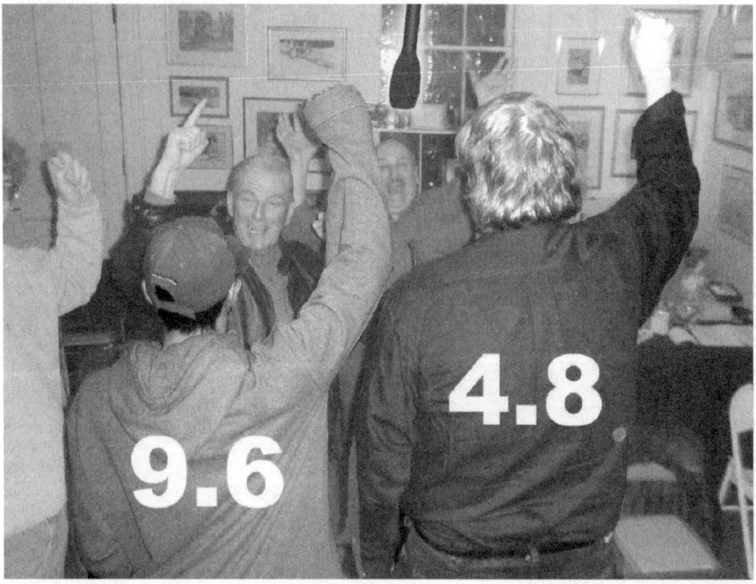

In the wake of a fallen sky

[02/25/02 @ 6:15pm]

at 3am I lie
comforting a lover I have already lost
to the truth
of our own ambivalence

tonight terror tightened
our hold

She could have
fallen from the 105th floor,
but time took her on tangents
that fills her now with tears instead

As I lie here comforting her,
I love another I lost before
the world showed us
that it cares less & more
than we thought

Feeling foreign with and without her
I comfort and console
without words;
my arms envelope
in ways my heart cannot

tightly wound
in our own worries
we lie
together
in separate spaces

It's a horrible time to have a hollow heart

It occurs to me
it is time to be true
so I wipe off tears
and say goodbye

Later this morning,
I send 18 roses to
my lost love

still not forgotten ❦

Let go
[03/20/02 @ 8:45pm]

Let go after
ten and a half years
he acknowledges
he hasn't worked
in a while

He hasn't worked
well
at seeing the
subtext
in his nine to five

Programming is not poetry

As daydreams
delayed
a future
founded in
uncertainty principals,
he forgot
his formula
for defining
his purpose

never in iambic,
never in rhyme

Let go
after ten and a half
he lets loose
becomes a poet

He makes more
with his mission to get people to publish private poetry

He makes poetry from PopTarts
and starts 2 say how simple it is
to finally see his syntax
can make sense

He finally finds out how clocks tick
forward
when
not still
not backward

Let go after ten and a half
he lets go
and gets going ❦

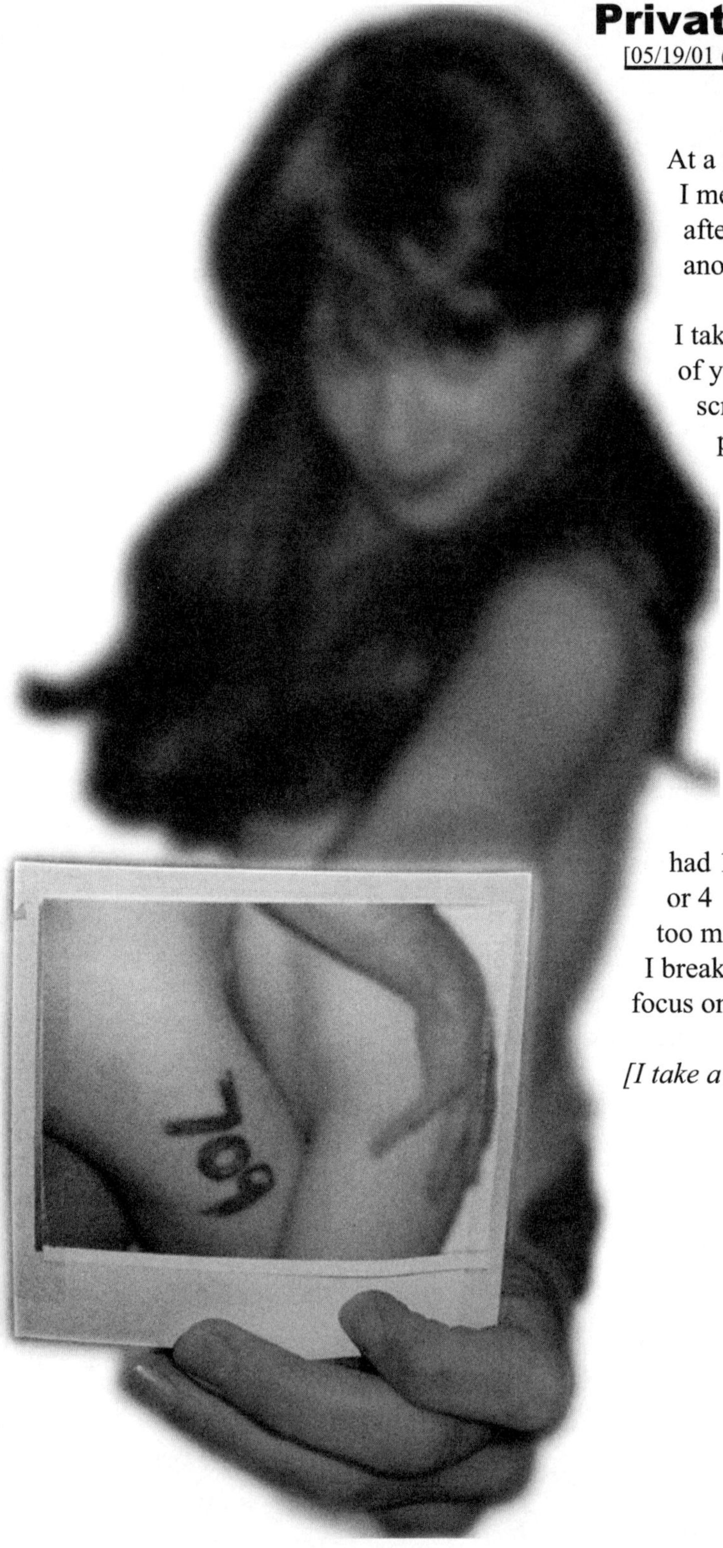

Private Polaroids

[05/19/01 @ 12pm]

At a friend's birthday party
I met you
after you were talking to
another guy

I take a private Polaroid
of you and him,
scratch him out,
paste myself in instead

It makes a
better picture

It's perfectly clear
I'll show you later
and take a new
Polaroid

A little later at the bar,
where we both have
had 1
or 4
too many shots,
I break convention,
focus on first kiss

[I take a private Polaroid] ❦

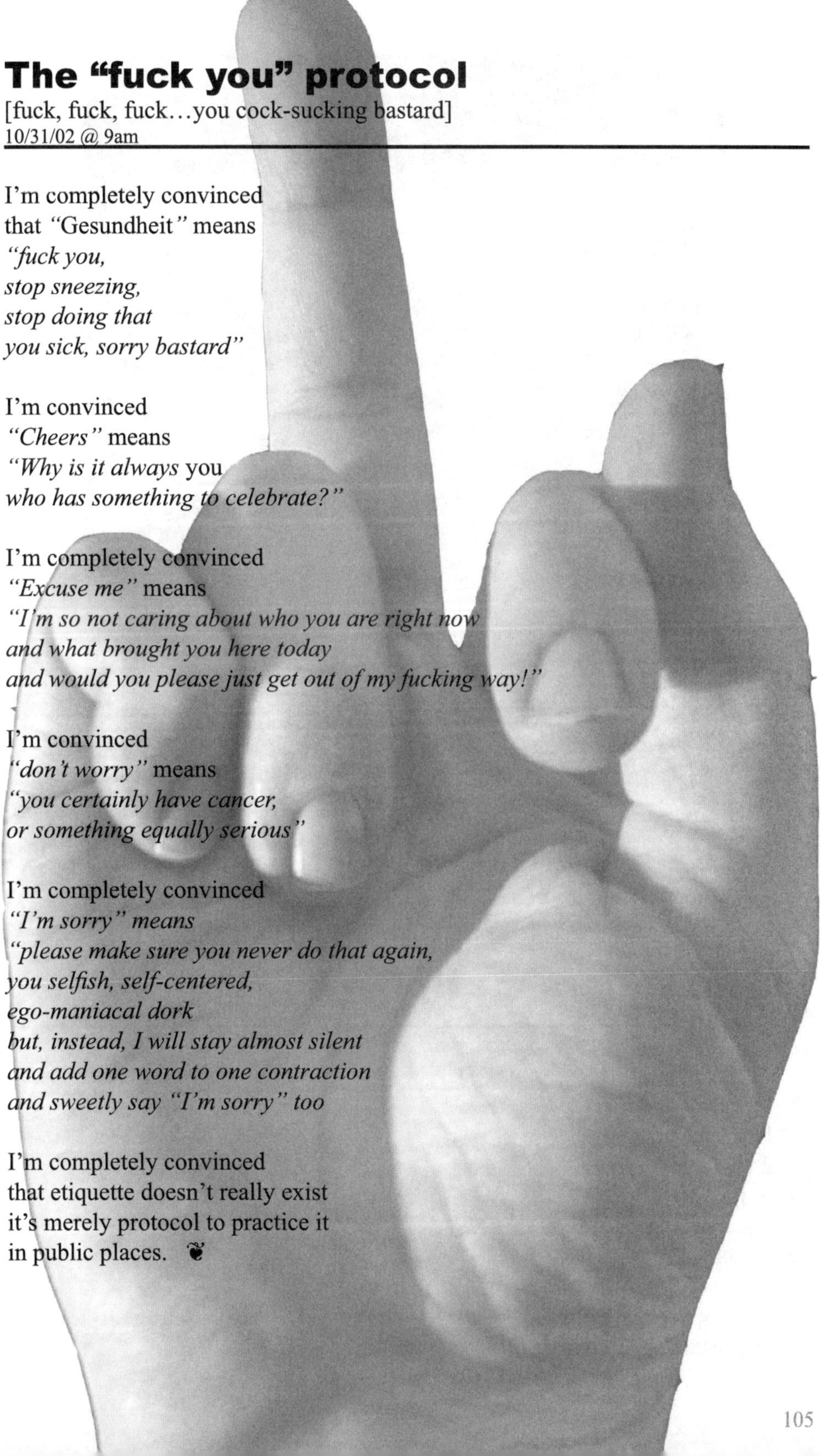

The "fuck you" protocol

[fuck, fuck, fuck…you cock-sucking bastard]
10/31/02 @ 9am

I'm completely convinced
that *"Gesundheit"* means
"fuck you,
stop sneezing,
stop doing that
you sick, sorry bastard"

I'm convinced
"Cheers" means
"Why is it always you
who has something to celebrate?"

I'm completely convinced
"Excuse me" means
"I'm so not caring about who you are right now
and what brought you here today
and would you please just get out of my fucking way!"

I'm convinced
"don't worry" means
"you certainly have cancer,
or something equally serious"

I'm completely convinced
"I'm sorry" means
"please make sure you never do that again,
you selfish, self-centered,
ego-maniacal dork
but, instead, I will stay almost silent
and add one word to one contraction
and sweetly say "I'm sorry" too

I'm completely convinced
that etiquette doesn't really exist
it's merely protocol to practice it
in public places. ❦

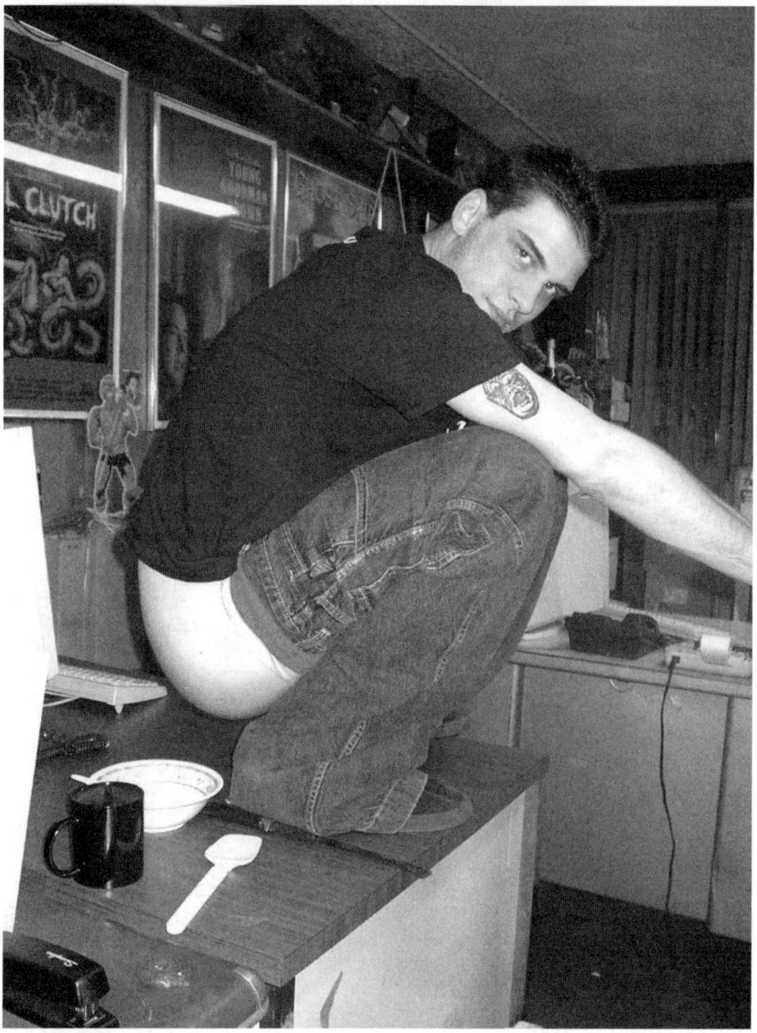

[John] Waters me up

[03/17/02 @ 5:40pm]

[Dear John, thanks for not being afraid to aggravate the uninitiated!]

Don't water me down
WATERS me up
Send me one dozen
PINK FLAMINGOS
to ponder as I play with my *PECKER*
and watch late night TV

Ain't free speech; artistic endeavors
and the fuckin' right to say *"fuck"* just for fuck sake

simply DIVINE?

Pathetically passionate about *POLYESTER* and *any* color but PURPLE,
please scratch as I sniff,
forget deodorant,
be pure & puerile

I *like* the way that I smell

Every adolescent urge
must be UN-endorsed
by colas & car companies
concerned with public perceptions
and social reflections

Truth rarely comes *"New & Improved"*
from the insecurity of aging
and the cowardice of compromise

Give me a six-pack
& let me tell you about my
MALE troubles
and let me dare to eat MY shit
before taking it from you

I have no patience for the *MONDO* mundane
just because I eat shit
don't think I'm insane
just a little bit tantalizingly *TRASHO*
for telling the truth

Don't water me down
WATERS me UP!!

Indulge me in aggravated indolence
I don't care to endear
just to be fuckin' sincere
don't water me down
WATERS me up!

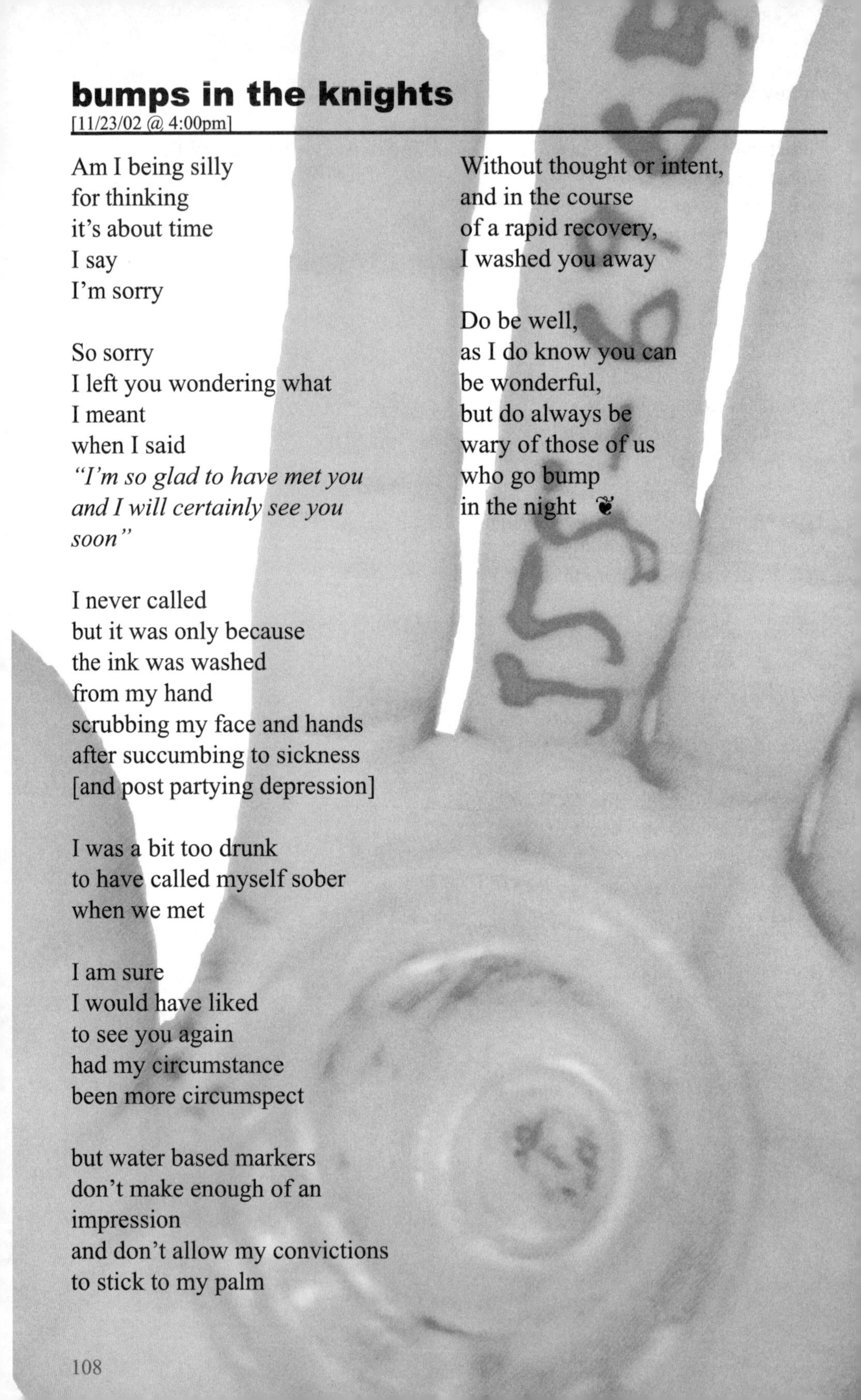

bumps in the knights

[11/23/02 @ 4:00pm]

Am I being silly
for thinking
it's about time
I say
I'm sorry

So sorry
I left you wondering what
I meant
when I said
*"I'm so glad to have met you
and I will certainly see you
soon"*

I never called
but it was only because
the ink was washed
from my hand
scrubbing my face and hands
after succumbing to sickness
[and post partying depression]

I was a bit too drunk
to have called myself sober
when we met

I am sure
I would have liked
to see you again
had my circumstance
been more circumspect

but water based markers
don't make enough of an
impression
and don't allow my convictions
to stick to my palm

Without thought or intent,
and in the course
of a rapid recovery,
I washed you away

Do be well,
as I do know you can
be wonderful,
but do always be
wary of those of us
who go bump
in the night ❦

I like the movies

[02/14/98 @ 12:20am]

I like the movies, let me explain.

She is so, so wet.
And it is because of me.

Her pants unzip down the back
so it is a difficult act of discretion to get them down to allow easy access.
I have only recently mastered this act.
Weeks ago this would never have been me.
I am learning fast.
I am such a romantic but this is just about pleasing my woman.
And sometimes her pleasure just can't wait.
And sometimes the dangers entice.

Shy I am, but excited I get.
She unzips and pulls me out.

A flashlight from behind gives us a scare
… but the usher must have another task.
An older couple sits 20 seats down in the same row… oblivious.
How exciting can this get?
We get to the point of no return.
And then release.
Our hands soaked.
Mine stays inside just a while longer.
… just lingering.
Her hand continues with a slow stroke.

Out in the open we both stay for a few minutes more.
Our hands drenched with no way to wipe.
So it's an air dry.
In the past few weeks this has become
a regular thing.

I like the movies.

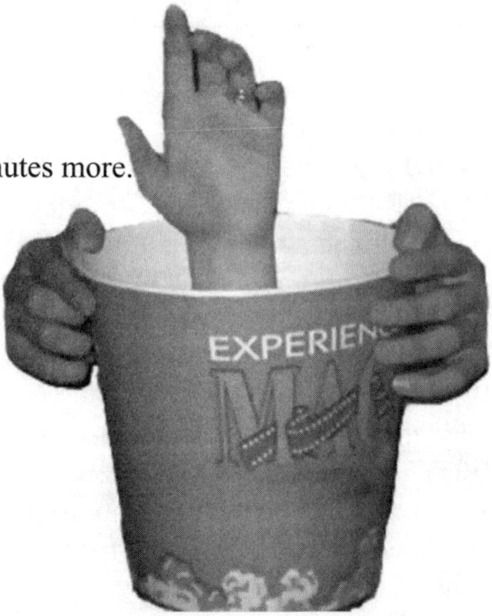

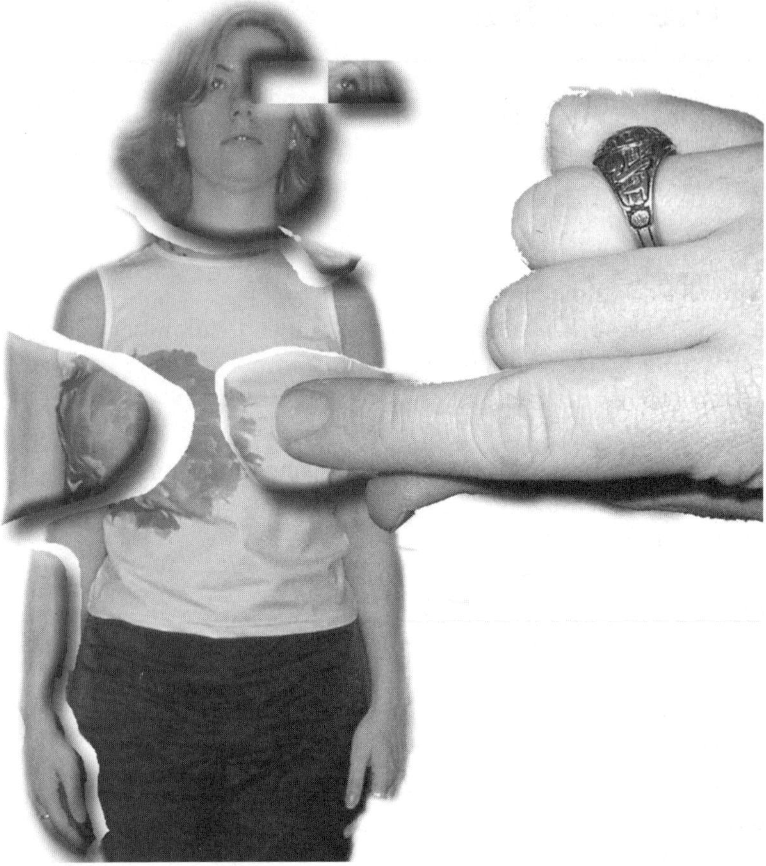

I want to puzzle you up

[09/20/00 @ 3:00am]

I want to UNteach you your simple geometry
to PUZZLE you down
RIDDLE you with moments of MOMENTUM
SQUARE your curves
bludgeon your softness into SUBMISSIVE aggressiveness

I need you to be on TOP BEGging to begin again on BOTTOM
I need to make you WONDER who I am
WHO you are
why you stay
WHY you can't leave
I want to answer all your questions with answers from DIFFERENT questions
soften your blade against my rock HARD
center
yourself

LOSE your direction
to THIS moment
in SEARCH of OUR next

Let's confuse and contradict ourselves
into square circles and
acutely angled sensations

Let's DISprove all our theorems of carnal cummings

TIE me down into your recessed cavities
of thought
into your BREATH

without a REASON, exhale into our passionate pose

Slide [this] up
glide [that] just left of epicenter
Let us TASTE TEST each other
unsolved and unsatisfied

only to repeat

Participate without patience

PAINT us together
in PIECES
paint us TOGETHER
in puzzled and staccato confusions of RAPTURE

Make THIS make sense
make NOW explode

ABANDON this second but not without promising the next

[*breathe*]

remind me of the voice and VICE or our VIRILITY

Sing me a LULLABY of consonants
save the VOWELS for bed ❦

It ain't me tonight

[06/16/99 @ 2:05pm]

It ain't me tonight,
on the 6:02 train from somewhere to *your* where,
it ain't me.

It ain't me waiting in your smile.

Ain't me in your dream last night,
in your bed tonight.

Ain't me you are missing now,
right now,
ain't me.

Ain't me.

Not me.

It isn't me.

It is NOT me.

IT IS NOT ME! ❦

Lady has a Secret

[January or February 1999]

Lady has a secret
a secret smile
a secret fear

Lady holds a tear
a tear for her
a tear for him

Lady has a smile
hidden in doubt

Lady has a scene
needs to *act* happy
to hold back the fear… hidden in a private tear… a soulful place

Force feed a smile
find the poetic peace in the pointless pain

I have a secret:
"Lady holds a home in my heart"

I have a secret

in a private tear ❦

Let the woman find me out

[04/07/99 @ 10:30am]

First dates, last dates… no dates.
Boring blind dates, unbearably unqualified dates.
Disastrously disinteresting and disinterested dates.
UNDER-interested me… UNDER-interested her.
Right times… wrong people.
Right places… wrong people.

-------- **Ambiguity. Confusion. Uncertainty.**

Should I hold her hand?

First date kisses
… or is that second date kisses?
Flowers, calls, candy.
Roses… yes roses
… or, no, a nice arrangement.
Will there be sex, can there be sex?
I like sex.
A lot!
Will there be love, can there be love?
I like love.
A lot MORE!
What does she want? What did she
want? What would she want?
… if she saw me?
… if she knew me?
… if she loved me?

Who is she?
-------- **Questions.**

Look here, now isn't she beautiful?
This one here.
There is *something* to her…
I can feel it. I think, I think… I can
KNOW it.
Does she look like she likes
looking at me?
Because I *do* like looking at her?
Be patient… take it slow… don't want
to scare away.
Be bold… take it fast
… don't want to seem disinterested.
She needs to feel the passion
… the potential for passion.

Do I turn her on?
She does turn me on.
She should turn me on.
Does she turn me on?

Maybe it's too fast.
Maybe it's too slow.
Maybe she's the one
Maybe she isn't.
Do I ask her out?
SHOULD I ask her out?
…
-------- **I'm tired.**

I'm tired of not knowing.

That look… she looked at me
… did you see?

What did that mean? WHAT the hell
did that mean!?

My eyes contact… dart away.

That was tough… so tough
… to see her… to see her.

Is she the one?

Fear of rejection.

Fear of acceptance.

What's the line… what's MY line?

How to approach

… and SHOULD I?

I pause, I look, I almost smile

… *almost*

I blink… look away.

What now I think?

Was that her?

Was that her? ❦

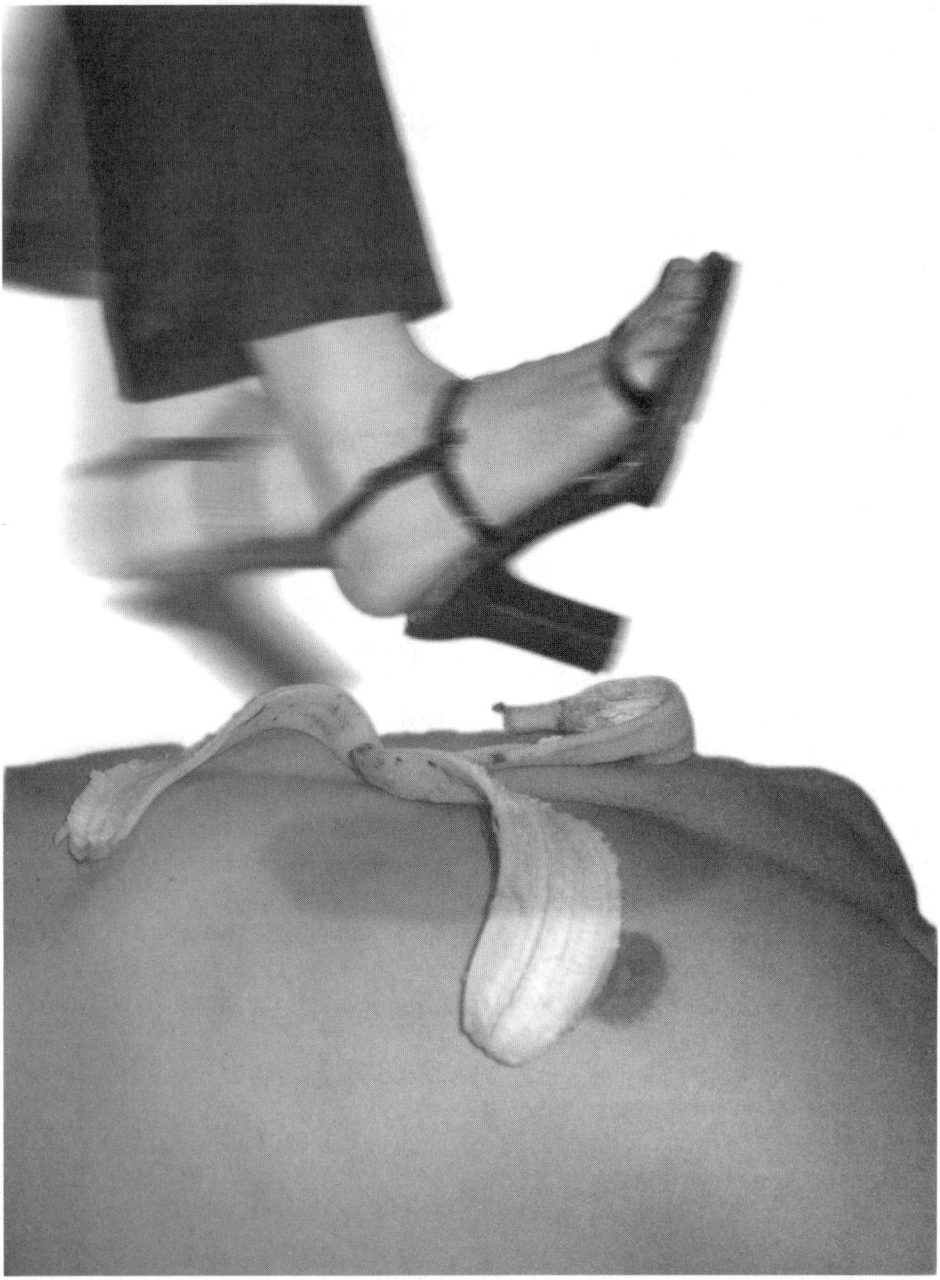

Let me slip your sideways

[Oct/Nov 2000]

into the recessed cavities of your carnal cautions
tracing curves with my mind
mind you not to lose balance
Please lose balance!
perchance to become an ornament
on my hood
take *this* train 'til it just doesn't stop
'til you need to come nowhere but back
after one last *"last call"*
come
and call me sexy
call me to surrender

tonight let us switch directions
map out a new geography
to *these* bodies

destination *everywhere*

Let's trace *all* our lips
until they voice new vocabularies of vice
it's so niiice to see you off track
you do disorient
my place of passion
I place a hand traveling due south
to the vertex of no one's undiscovered country
don't doubt its destination
that delights in getting lost
and getting there luxuriously
late

late in each other's rapture ❦

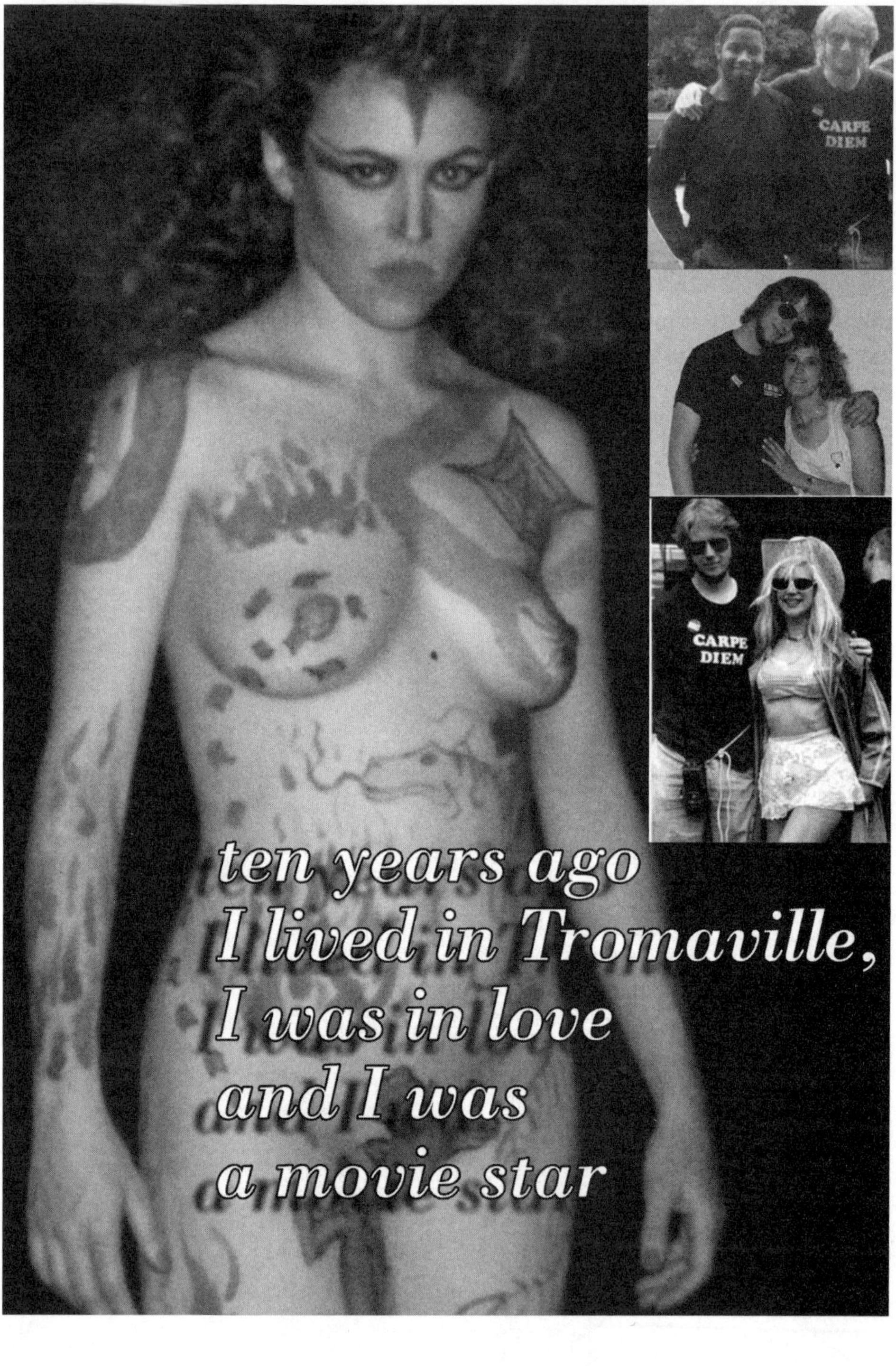
CARPE DIEM
CARPE DIEM
ten years ago
I lived in Tromaville,
I was in love
and I was
a movie star

Lost & Found in Tromaville

[05/02/97 @ 4:17am]

I was lost.

"More limbs, I need more limbs... get more limbs in there!" Lloyd screams.

Terry, the script supervisor, sworn to the duty of continuity of details, says, "But Lloyd, you have three shots in the can that won't match."

"Thank you for your input, Terry, but this is Tromaville," Lloyd says.

Terry starts, *"But Lloyd, my job is..."*

"More limbs. It's Tromaville! Get some hands... and a few heads in there!"

For the overhead shot there simply has to be more carnage... this is a *Troma* picture after all... there are standards of carnage to be upheld.

And, in Tromaville, there really is no such thing as continuity. Lloyd aims above the details.

Lloyd is one of those truly brilliant people. It's not just that he is a Harvard or Yale graduate [one of those super-duper Ivy league schools]. It's not just that he has built an incredibly successful business. It is just that he is Lloyd... part maniac, part philosopher and the rest only God knows what.

He's a man that can yell really loud if it suits his fancy. But he can also talk about Nietzche. My mother likes him a whole lot. She has never seen him yell, but she has talked philosophy with him. If he is a maniac, he certainly is a charming one. I like him too. And I respect him even more. I don't know why and that must be exactly the reason.

Moments before we blew up a house. I thought I knew what the "Big Bang" was, but until you have blown up a house you really don't know the meaning.

Running around like a madman I hand out one hundred earplugs. Speaking with a strange Swedish accent, I repeat to all on set: "Earplugs for big bang… big, big boom… must wear ear plug thing-a-ma-jigs."

I had never needed earplugs in the past, but when you blow up a house it is a good idea. Trust me.

Don't ask me why I started using a Swedish accent on this day… but it would be a few months before I lost it. I think the accent came with the job.

It's my first day on set. It's my first major motion picture. This is what I went to school for… to help blow up buildings and get more body parts inside the circle of thugs trying to kill the mutated super-hero from New Jersey.

Toxic Avenger Part II is the name of the picture… if you are truly cultured then you know what I'm talking about… if not, then maybe you should expand your horizons.

Troma changed my life. It was a long time ago… about 10 years.

I always knew I wanted to work in the movies. With a degree in Broadcast & Film from Boston University in hand I hit the New York City pavement knocking on every door trying to get work on some big boring commercial as a geeky gopher getting this or that for him, her, or it. Because that is what film school graduates do.

I really wasn't thinking straight then.

You see, I love movies. I mean I LOVE movies!!

A couple days after blowing up the house we are shooting in a park in Peekskill. I am standing around waiting to be told to fetch this or fetch that.

I truly was a loyal and faithful production assistant.

Lloyd yells out to me, *"Zork, go sit on the steps over there and, you know, look homeless."*

It's been a bad casting day, things are *way* behind schedule and in Tromaville that is normal but just won't do. There is supposed to be a caravan of homeless people, but none were brought in from New York with the busload of extras today, so Lloyd sends me in along with a local Peekskill lady to fill up the shot.

Set locked, slate slapped.

Camera rushes in and Lloyd says, *"Zork, say something."*

"What should I say, Lloyd?"

"I don't know, anything... say, 'Mom, who are these people?'"

"OK, roll camera."

Flustered, confused and nervous I blurt out five simple words.

"Let's get one for safety," Lloyd says. And I repeat my five words.

"Cut. Print. Wrap. Let's move on, we're losing the light."

Right then and there Lloyd made me a movie star. Minutes before I was an unknown bumbling P.A. and now I had my five seconds of fame.

A year later Mario Van Peebles [some called him "Sunny Spoon" and some didn't] will say the same thing to me on a completely different shoot. "Zork, get over there and look homeless."

I hope it's just a symptom of not combing my hair enough and not foreshadowing.

I'm sure one day film scholars will find phenomenal symbolism in the dialog of my scene. And I'm sure one day they will appreciate the subtle nuances of my powerful performance.

But at this moment it was time to get back to my P.A. duties. I went back to getting this and that for him, her, and it.

I had been silly when I thought of working on commercials… and I must have been mad when I went to work for Troma.

Months before this madness, after my first commercial job offer I had called up Troma and asked if they were looking for any help. And the conversation that ensued is as follows:

Man on the phone says, *"You don't want to work here!"*

"Yes, I do," I say.

"Trust me, you don't. We work you like a dog and yell at you a lot. REALLY, you don't want to work here!"

"Whatever doesn't kill me makes me stronger… and I used to have a cat," I say.

"We pay you next to nothing. You DON'T want to work here."

"Art rarely pays. I DO want to work for Troma."

We fought about this for a while… I won.

Troma has really odd recruiting methods… but they work.

For twelve weeks, six days a week, 16 hours a day I was immersed in Tromaville. Dickens wrote about a best of times/worst of times scenario… I am sure he must have worked for Troma.

But mostly, it was the best of times. If you don't mind bypassing the luxuries of normal life like sleep, sex & and a firm financial foundation then Tromaville is a great place to live for a while.

I now had daily duties on the shoot. I was the go-getter Production Assistant and every time the good people of Tromaville are needed I would rub dirt on my face, put on a stupid hat and grin and get in front of the camera.

Frequently I would get beat up with a loaf of bread… by Mike Tyson, no less. Actually it is the HBO version of Mike Tyson. Oops, no it was Spawn that beat me up. Actually it was Michael Jai White and, as a running gag, every chance he would get, he would take the loaf of bread I had waiting for him in my shopping cart and hit me over the head with it. How many people can say they have been beaten up with loafs of bread by Spawn… or was that Mike Tyson?

And then I got to watch Arthur, the lucky British FX guy, paint this lovely naked lady. I am not sure why she has to be naked or why she was adorned with these illustrations, but I can hardly say I object. And, after all, this is Tromaville.

I wanted Arthur's job.

In between shots I hang out with my fellow Production Assistants. And here I am with Kuzy… I love her… just look and I am sure you can tell.

She doesn't know so let's keep it our small secret. I have never told her, I have never kissed her… and I never even tried. Certain dreams are better off left that way.

That way they can stay with you forever.

Isn't she something, though? Just look at that smile and look carefully at what's right behind those eyes… you'll fall in love with her too.

But remember she was my dream first.

Oh, and look here. Here I have my arms wrapped around Phoebe… she's Toxie's girlfriend. But he's not jealous. I am not a threat. She really doesn't like me anyway… just take a look at that patronizing grin.

But who cares! I already have MY dream!

In a few seconds, if I remember right, I have to run off down the street to pick up a dozen pizzas. These film crews get pretty unruly if you don't feed them.

So, now I snap back to present day… the here and ho-hum now. I am as far away from an artistic life as possible. I program computers and make about a billion times more money than I did back then.

But I haven't gotten to blow up any houses recently, and Spawn hasn't beaten me up with French bread in almost a decade. I never order more than one pizza at a time.

Most people would say it is crazy. But ten years ago I lived in Tromaville, I was in love and I was a movie star.

Today… right now… I am in love, I am a movie star and I am in Tromaville.

Lloyd yells, *"Agra, agra!!!"* Whatever that means.

I am found.

[Thanks Troma.] ❦

LOOK
AT ME.
LOOK
AT WHAT
I CAUGHT.

Look at what I caught

[04/18/98 @ 1:12am]

Look at me, I am so, so proud.
Look at what I caught.
It is such a gloriously sunny day on the Long Island sound.
The clouds above could be served as cotton candy at the Yonkers County Fair.
And such a big fish… such a beautiful fish… I caught it.
I wear a grin that is almost demonically goofy.
I have so much to smile about.

This truly is a great day.
I really am quite the fisherman… just look at my Marlen's fins
That stranger walking behind me, he is in awe of what I have caught.

Look at my wife, isn't she beautiful?
She's a model, you know?
She's a *Ford* model… not just any model.

She stands with me with such beauty and grace.
And that makes me stand so tall… 6'4" tall… because of her, I think.
She was an A.B.T. Dancer.
Such grace… such beauty… held within my arms.

Look at what I caught
… such a beautiful woman
… such a graceful, bright and beautiful woman!

I can't even begin to imagine how I lured her into my arms.

She put me through medical school with her dancing and modeling.

Someday soon she will give all that up to mother a couple children for us.

Two boys, yes, two boys I want.

But we have time… we are still young.

Look at the way she smiles when she is in my arms
… and look at my smile
… the smile that grows from knowing I can make her this happy.

I smile knowing that someday soon I will have two special sons.

One will master computers and science… he'll go to MIT and program space satellites or something like that.

Our second son will grow up to be an artist of sorts… maybe a part-time poet who will express the kinds of things I never could.

Maybe one day he will write about the sons I will never get to see grow up.

He'll grow up to write about how proud I am of what they have become … even if I am not around to see it.

He'll write about how proud I am of my beautiful wife who will give them all the love I won't be able to. He'll write about how proud we all are when she becomes President of Bonds & Arbitrage at her bank.

I married such a bright woman. She gave up college for me… to help put me through school, but I am sure she will graduate one day Suma Cum Laud… she is just that smart!

Look at me… look at that smile… I am so proud of the things that I will never get to see and the family I won't get to nurture.

I already miss the ball games and man-to-man talks and the first-date coachings and so many other things I won't be able to share with my sons. But I will always love them so much… even when I won't be around to let them know.

But my family will remember me and how proud I am of them.

Can't you see my smile? ❦

Turning out the lights

[05/11/2000 @ 2:46am]

In the dark you don't dare rhyme.

Was it your storm? Did you plan it this way?

I listen to your stories,

small talk turned large,

poetry by candlelight,

naughty and nice,

wanting to kiss,

who's to stop us now? ❦

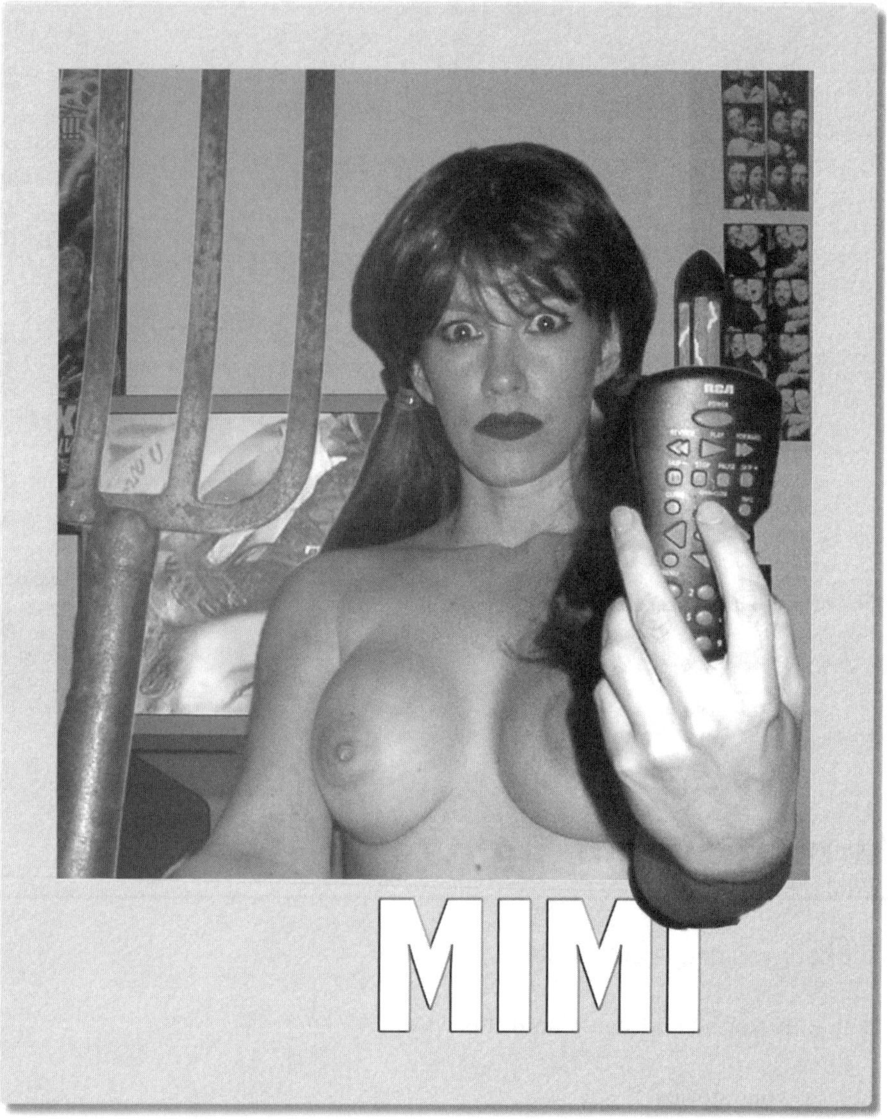

[photos by author / model = Debbie Rochon (www.debbierochon.com)]

Mammaries of a Missed Mimi
[a.k.a.: a totally untrue tale told by trailer trash]

[02/27/02 @ 8:30pm]

Built like a Botticelli, she was big & busty
in a beee-aaa-uuu-ti-ful way
in an *almost* slender way
in an only *sort of* beer bellied kind of way
and had quite a butt to boot

Her mammaries are mountainous
& I miss them much

The way she used to saunter
over to me
staying sexy & doing a simple striptease
while I watched TV

"Whoo"-followed-by an-*"ahh!"*
"WHOO-----ahhhhh!!!"

She would tease me totally before touching me
& let me tell you
the tip of her tongue was *tremendously* talented too

Early in the evening she
would invite me over
to watch *Mr. Ed* or such on the *E* channel

In college, for extra cash, she modeled nude
for artistic academics
because she liked the look of herself
in other people's paints

So, in front of the TV, naughtily nude, she acts out her favorite bits during the commercial breaks and this makes me enormously erect

But then,
during the final acts
she stands right in front
of the TV and starts singing a show tune,
a *different* show tune,

an *annoying* show tune,
I mean something like *Green Acres*

This annoys me entirely!

Like Mars Blackmon on a sugar rush
I go, *"Please baby, please baby, please*
can't you slide yourself just 6 or so inches to the left or right
so I can see the TV"
but, needless to say, *she's gotta have it*
when she wants it
and now she is having *show tunes*.
not Broadway… but like *Nick @ Night* show tunes

But she is nude
and this makes me much more motivated,
helps get me hot & horny,
completely conflicting my challenging cable TV conundrum
of tuning into the tube

So I forgive and forget

Her standing there
evokes all my
ogling instincts

I sit here
on a big black leather couch
remote in one hand, dick in the other
erect and ogling

I wonder how I will manage to get my beer when I need a sip

You see, she is quite well endowed in an un-enhanced kind of way
& her nipples stand erect
… and so do I
only I am still sitting down

I am not sure if she is more turned on by my erection
or her own singing
but what do I care
sometimes her ends justified all her means

and, hell, we are both right here

and it *is* a commercial break

By now, we both have time to distract each other
for at least 2 minutes more before the next show starts

…

But that sexy scene
was six months ago
and it's been many moons
since I have molded Mimi's mammaries
in my mitts

She is gone now

Quite seriously gone now

It's a sad, sad fact that she left me flat on April Fool's day
making me wonder if it was a joke she never let herself in on

TV has never really been the same since

And now I have show tunes in my head

I am missing Mimi's mammaries much!!

And I am all too aware that, right now,
Green Acres is the place to be ❦

11
12
1
10
2
9
3
8
4

Moments in the Dark

[6/14/97 @ 9:17am]

I am looking straight into her eyes in the dark… I can't really see them but that is where I am looking.

After dinner, in the restaurant parking lot, at this late hour, holding hands, I make sure not to count the minutes.

We have code words… *"red wine"... "private dancing."*

Tonight we will drink, we will dance.

Our hands clasp; our fingers caress; then they make love.

On the radio Ivan Neville sings *"I don't want to grow up"* and *"Stay what you are."*

We don't grow up. Instead, we stay here and hold.

She straddles my lap,
and comes in for an extended session of kissing
… European style.

I kiss her neck. She quivers.

Tonight we will drink each other. We will dance decadently.

She sits back in the passenger seat and we clasp hands again.

Here and now is *special.*

Our eyes blindly connect… connecting in the dark we see what's behind the silence & inside our blackness. Light would only cloud our vision & distract the distance we displace with wine… with dance… in these moments in the dark.

I appreciate these uncounted moments, moments in the dark, holding hands, looking into her eyes that I can't quite see. ❦

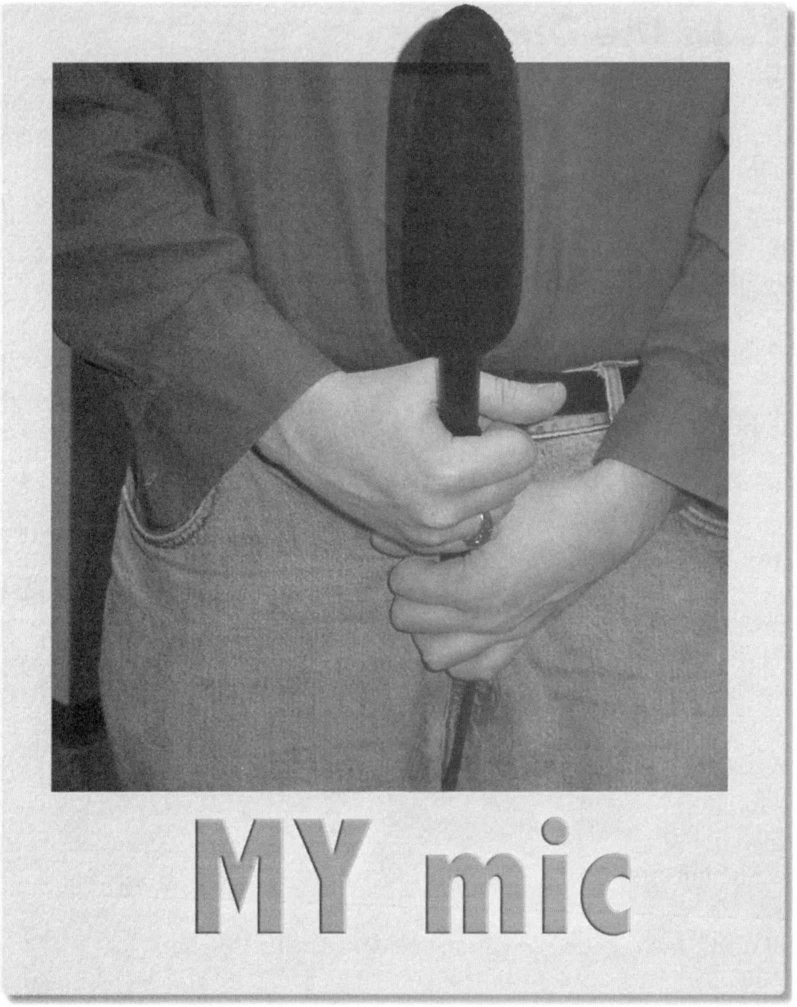

my mic
[07/03/02 @ 9:00pm]

this is *my* microphone
to do with as I please

you have nothing to say about it

at least for 3 minutes,

till I'm done with my Dunkin Donuts
till the tap is changed
and my Bud is back
where it belongs

right here!

this is *my* microphone

till you settle down
till you stop talking
till you listen up

till that fight out back stops

or this one in the corner starts

till your girlfriend stops bitching
about you being late tonight

till you forget that
you KNOW she faked it
last night

my mic
till I turn u on
enough to ask me out

don't worry I have some
time left to wait
for you to come
to your senses

this is *my* mic, till you young man
stop picking your nose
didn't your mommy tell you
never to pick your nose?
… *in public*
you know, where people
can *see* you

the trick is to dip your
head into your hand and
cover your face, like in a cough,
then swing thumb inside & out in
one swift scoop

or, if you like to be particular perverse
in public,
then just pretend a hacking cough
and go crazy picking out plenty

or, better yet, do it while driving

it's a well known fact that
nose picking doesn't count as a
social sin at speeds exceeding
45 miles per hour

this is *my* microphone
to do with as I please
you having *nothing* to say about it

I might choose to talk
about my stock portfolio
and give you a few tips

although I'd have to warn you
about ever taking financial advice from
a *poet*

for Christ's sakes… it's an *open* mic
and we're all here
instead of being
well, you know,
like over there

there where
they stay (for all practical purposes)
silent
and sip champagne
at cocktail parties
with foo-foo things
like
"es carts-go" and pigs in a blanket
over there where they talk in
hushed tones
afraid someone
might notice
they're *lying through their teeth*
when they say they
made money in "arb-i-trage"

vote their conscience

like David Lynch films

when they say
that they are… happy

no, that's not for me,
I rather be here
broke, kind of bored,
a little bit constipated
from bad Chinese take-out today
and *berate* them
[I just looked up that word *"berate"* in

my dictionary, it's in between
"bequest" and *"Berber"* and it is by far
the best of the bunch]

No, I'd rather be here
standing tall
sipping Dunkin Donuts
not that swanky Starbucks stuff,
not that flavored crap
just regular 24 oz. super sized
Dunkin Donuts

I'd rather stand here sipping
waiting for my beer to come
from the back

this is *my* microphone
to do with as *I* please

I can bore you again and *again* about
1st kisses that seem to never, ever stop
being
so, so sappy

until the girl dumps me, that is
then I'll bitch and bitch about that
"never was no good" bitch
that broke my heart

again and again, I'll bitch

MY microphone

I can make funny sounds
["eh-he-eh-he-eh-he-fuurrrr"]

I can talk about sex

this is *my* microphone

I can talk about politics
tell you Ronald Reagan
ruled righteously
and church *should* have
a synchronicity with state

and both Bushes are the best

I'd be lying
but I have the right
to get a rise from you

this is *my* mic
I'll sing out of tune
maybe talk about
my mutual movie theater
masturbations

this is *my* mic
to rhyme,
or,
better yet,
NOT

this is MY microphone,
this is MY microphone,
THIS IS MY MICROPHONE!!!!

[BUZZZZZZZZ]

Ooops, I almost forgot

This is *your* microphone

say whatever *you* need to say

I've got a beer to get back to

Please keep me entertained,
but for no more than 3 minutes ❦

Boy/Girl Kind of Thing

[04/08/97 @ 2:30am**]

I am looking for a boy/girl kind of thing

the kind of thing you so often find in high school

the kind of thing with innocence in *almost* everything

where nothing is taken for granted

holding hands, soft caresses, simple sloppy kisses

honesty in innocence,
grace in awkwardness,
truth in discovery

I am looking for the boy/girl kind of thing
where every moment re-invents a smile

where the richness of the *sharing* makes the world a truly *richer* place

I am looking for the boy/girl kind of thing you see in the movies
guaranteed to make a pair of young lovers smile ❦

no poem tonight
[04/17/02]

I won't be writing a poem tonight
so slide close,
slide swift,
stay sweet,
and kiss me

I won't let you be sorry

We'll sift through our breaths
to a simpler seduction when
we didn't worry about
pentameter passions

We'll leave the audience unaware

I won't be writing a poem
about our first kiss
and how we explore
cavernous concerns
of chemistry, caring
and third-date rules

Tell me a secret
make it special
I'll keep it close
and hold you closer

I won't write tonight

Let's let *this* last
as we learn to love again
without the registry of language

Let's learn to love again
before we take notes
and stack the nights into
sentence structures

And I drop my pens and let you in

We begin again
without the cursive concerns

Just you and I
us three alone
will learn to love
without the rhyme
just you and I
just us three alone

I won't write about
any of it at all
just slide on close
and kiss me deep

I drop my pen
and show you I am *write* here ❦

past imperfect

[01/18/03 8pm]

Instead of starting
with present tense
you revise our work
to the beginning of our end

You circle some spots
you see and say
it's the absolute completion
of a past imperfect

your sentence starts with a period
and my pronouns are not invited
to participate in your poetry

you leave me with only
pause enough
to pen this poem
about past participles
and misplaced
parts of speech

So, I stand here
and listen for you
back in this present tenseness
with your affinity
for proper punctuation ❦

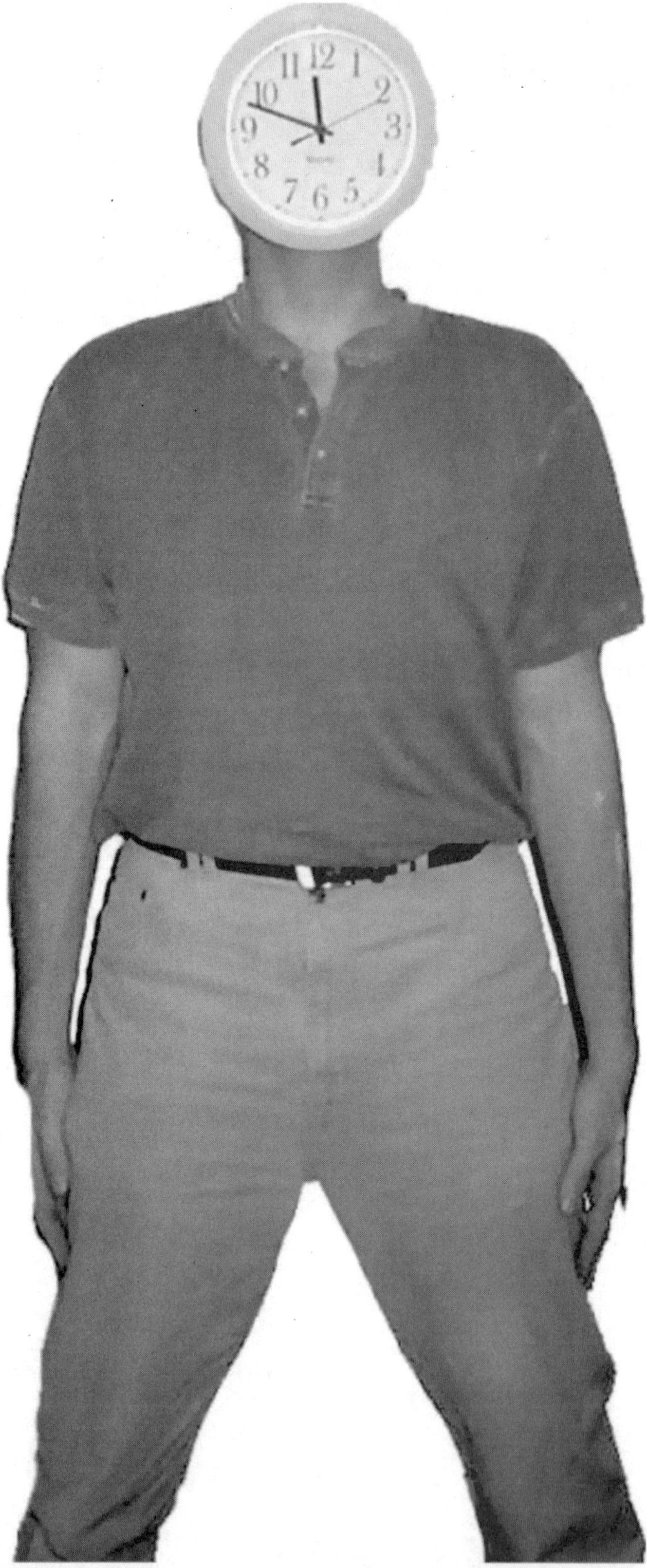

Now that ended too soon

[02/09/98 @ 9pm]

"Now that ended too soon," she says.
It's a first date, although I would never guess that.
We both are more comfortable than we have any reason to expect.

She impresses me more at dinner.
She's beautiful, bright and *quite* unique.
Discretely she steals food from my plate and words from my mouth.

"Let's keep this simple," we say.
"Let's start this sexy," we think.

She steals food, words, and thoughts and we *are* comfortably sexy.

Out in the parking lot she says, *"I'll give you a good night hug."*
And this we do.
The light goes out, just as we start to part.
The new lighting strikes her fancy.
"Now, I'll give you a kiss good night."
And this we do.

In the singular sensation of one careful kiss… we make love

First kisses are an awkward thing
I don't overstay my welcome.
although amazingly aroused, I pull away.

"Now that ended too soon," she says.

We part as I still hold onto the tips of her fingers in my outstretched hand.
I want to pull her back into my arms for some more.

Now that ended too soon. ❦

1 year = 10,000 tears

1,000 kisses = 1 µ=miss

me – µ ═══ [so] blµe

2 people + 1 dream :: 8

kiss/(miss)

=

love/dove

Lover NOT= love
OR
Lover = love
If µ d-cide to c me
We will C
Then 1,000 dreams dance

hot date/ (lµstful) state

Numerology and bad rhyming schemes

[03/31/2000 @ 12:27am]

I fell in love with Jen 1,165 days after our first snowball fight.

It was 2 weeks after I met her that we first fought
... with snow.

For the first 14 days she had annoyed me… she was the bad guy [alt: bad gal].

My then new [and later ex] stepsister quite simply ticked me off. She was the enemy. At 13 I wasn't looking for any new friends. I most certainly wasn't looking to fall in love.

I wasn't looking for two new stepsisters.

On that 14th day of knowing Jen [which was 1,164 days before loving], Beth, the older sister by 391 days, was my ally. She served a purpose.

It was 2 against 2. Beth(14) & I(13) against my brother(15) & Jen(12) in a snowball fight to the death.

I took this all 2 seriously then.

And, now that I think about it, I take it 2 seriously now.

But back then I was much wiser.

Wisdom in simplicity. You see, I wasn't counting then.

I wasn't in love then.

Beth and I built up a small fortress wall of snow that stretched for 4 feet 3 inches wide and 15 inches tall.

It was a long snowball fight and we built this in turns while we protected each other.

Once the wall was built, we hid behind it and started rolling balls of ammunition.

My brother and Jen carelessly threw snowballs into our wall.

Beth & I stockpiled.

When a proper stash was built up, I took 5 balls and ran quick and fast up to Jen and in 1 rapid fire sequence I clobbered her.

Who would have thought that 166.42 weeks later, when 17, I would fall in love with her on the 9th hole of a miniature golf course.

…

We were on windmill hole #8…
I was losing terribly
… and I did not mind at all.

And, mind you, I was not losing on purpose. Jen was winning with an all 2 natural & dramatic lead. Her 17 to my 26.

While this was a par 4 hole I was already on my 7th stroke.

As soon as we got to the 9th hole, I knew I was in love.

My mother got divorced from my [now ex] step-dad exactly 1 year and 27 days after they had married when I was 13. So Jen was only my "sort-of-sister" for 392 days. We saw each other for 2 of every 14 days throughout that year. For[4] 4 years, twice every year, I drove 282.45 miles to drive by my old home, school, and, of course, go to the mall.

And 2 visit Jen.

I never visited Beth. Us younger siblings had to stick together.

Or maybe there was another reason that hadn't FORMULATED itself yet.

On that last hole of miniature golf it all became clear.

Jen was winning… and [competitive me] was smiling. I was actually rooting for her.

It's a sad matter of record, history and fact that I never kissed Jen. I never even tried.

…

In the years since I have done EVERYTHING but fall in love again.

I have had 47.5 first dates. I have had 6 lovers.

I have dated 1 Delicious Dell,
a Tasty Texan from North of the BORDER
who needed to take 8 pills a day to fight 1 bipolar DISORDER.

With ONE twenty ONE, just for FUN, Tarty teacher
I had 1 kiss and 1 DATE.
That did, indeed, put us both in quite a lustful STATE.
But when all revved up and with no place to STAY,
in 120 hours, she quickly, and quite simply, ran AWAY.

Trust me on her numbers, I double checked her math.

It took me 2 dates to kiss the Beautiful Brazilian 3 times while her Aunt peaked through the window LIGHT.
On the 2nd time we parked the car clean out of SIGHT.
And by the 3rd time we spent all NIGHT.

I've had 20 kisses in each and every hour with 1 21 year old who was merely 5 feet TALL.
By the time she GREW TO 22 we kissed not at ALL.

Trapped by an IQ of 150,
with her passion she was on again, off again THRIFTY.

$397 dollar phone BILL
did little good proving her romantic good WILL.

I felt USED and ABUSED… really quite RUDE.

Indeed, this was all a massive REDUCTION from her twilight SEDUCTION.

But still, I'd say to her again and again *"Let's K.I.S.S.,"*
hopelessly hoping it's the acronym *"Keep it SIMPLE Silly"* she would not MISS.

She might as well have been 80
since her thoughts were so, so WEIGHTY.

Romance Removed, Passion Perused.

With 2 women I have shared at least 40 orgasms in
very public PLACES.
I have made love in some pretty wild SPACES.

Acting Amanda initiates improvised naughtily naked REHEARSAL.
Terrible timing sends sexy script into 2nd act romantic REVERSAL.

Only ONCE I kissed my 3X a lady when outside her front DOOR.
8 months later I masturbated her on the dance FLOOR.

2 times I have broken hearts when love wouldn't COME.
It is never easy to say "goodbye" when all has been said and DONE.

Only once more I suffered a broken HEART.
It was the result of a 144th carefully misplaced Pop TART.

After 8 dates my one REMISS
is that I never even tried to KISS.

Her love I found & LOST,
leaving my heart with quite a freeze-dried FROST.
...
Stop the math... stop the COUNTING.
There is nothing left to rhyme when all is trapped in DOUBTING.

On a soapbox I stand and am numb from all the NUMBERS.
We are all too trapped in our romantically riddled SLUMBERS.

A romantic I am, but the heart has no place for MATH.
1 step at a time I will find my own PATH.

But, today [and right now], I think I will RELAX.
This rhyming scheme is so simple that I may even take a BATH.

I'll fill it with BUBBLES and pop away all my TROUBLES.

My only PLAN will be to find my next KISS.
It is all too true that the numbers I won't MISS.

Take these 7 tips:
==
1.) Do NOT look for love
just take the moments as they come

2.) Do not count the DAYS
just listen to what she SAYS

150/thrifty
room/gloom
reduction/seduction
80/weighty
tommorow/sorrow
how/now
later/date her
i+u=2+;)

You will find the answers in the here & now
to expect much more is, quite simply, DUMB
life will teach you what you can and will BECOME

3.) Whatever it takes make sure you don't get trapped by a DREAM
It's clearly as bad to do as this rhyming SCHEME.

4.) Life is so simple.

Life is so SIMPLE!

Why not treat it that WAY?

5.) Take each moment day by DAY.

Keep up the rhythm but stop the damn RHYME.

6.) It is time just to take your own sweet TIME.

…
…

So there I was at 17 on the ninth hole.

I wasn't counting. I wasn't planning… but I was in love with the *simplicity* of that moment and her sweet smile.

It is such a simple life. Why bother counting the holes till you find it all?

Just kiss her. Just kiss the GIRL.
Surely, surely, this will take your spirit for a pleasant WHIRL.

When you get right down to it, it's not even about finding the love.

The beauty is in the moment.

Thinking of TOMMOROWS will only usher SORROWS.

Romance is about HOW you taste the here and NOW.

Resist the counting, let the love find YOU LATE-ER.

But for right now… for RIGHT now… just DATE-HER. ❦

let me count the ways

If I were a songwriter
I would write you a song
sappy enough
to make most people sick.

If I were a caveman
I would etch you upon
my stone walls
and retrace
your curves
all winter long

If I were a trash man
I would bring you home the
finest relics
abandoned
on the edges of people's past;
orphaned
with beauty
that only you and I could see
for certain

If I were a cement worker
I would do
my best to make a more
permanent impression
on your sidewalk
and lay my heart down
in a sort-of-stony way
for you to step upon
on your way home
each night

If I were a gynecologist
I would bronze your best parts
and mount them above my
mantel, just so I can show you off
to company
when serving dessert

If I were a poet
I would edit this poem
now
to something like,
something like,
two syllables or less

just you and me
just u & me ❦

~~*[But I am a poET*~~
~~*and, although sometimes*~~
~~*I know IT,*~~
~~*I blow IT*~~
~~*when I try to show IT*~~
~~*off]*~~
(editor's note: Zork, stop being stupid!)

a poet's promise

I will break you
with lines
and miss all your metaphors,
slip all over your sestinas,
punctuate you improperly,
strip you of your
stanza breaks

If I were to try a sonnet
I would screw myself up, but only
because my passion keeps pushing my
pen into
all your unruly places ❦

[Have I told you how much
I love your ligatures?]

TiVo poem

(to see the TiVo winning poem go to www.stolensnapshots.com)

I won a TiVo™ with a poem-
and now I digitally record
romantic movies
and study the moves
of Mel
and memorize Spacey's syntax

And at 2 am I use my TiVo
to shift my higher learning
onto the art of loving
learned from pirated Playboy

Good thing I had studied
up with the TiVo
late, late at night:

When faced
with a naked brunette
with a taste for my so-called
talent,
it all paid off

Yes, it's a good thing I had studied
up with the
TiVo
late, late at night:

Whoever told you poetry
doesn't pay
doesn't know shit! ❦

a work of art

I start at the top
and work my way
down

Down to
concealed centers wanting
more of my
attention;
more
investigation

Stopped in the
beauty,
penitent,
I pay proper attention
to all these telling
details

the rippled waves;
the marks of moisture;
the spots of
improvisation

After careful consideration
I see
it's time to change the
sheets ❦

Acute Angles

It's done weekly
when I decide
it's time to practice more

I've studied the training tapes,
mastered the manual,
and tried a terrible amount of
techniques

I'm careful with
inserting proper
punctuation
and completely careful with
all the acute angles of our
geometry

I aim to be
always aware
and avoid all our obtuse
instincts

I can't say I have mastered much
but I sure do
like to
study ❦

ooh baby, baby

[01/25/01 @ 2:20pm]

Kiss me in 1 syllable or less

if you hold me… you can have me

always searching

looking within each broken breath
for a place to interrupt
all within 32 words or less
between the breath in and the breath out
All within 46 words or less
… because, with you,
I just need the extra time ❦

Push Up Poem

I
This is my push up
poem

II
It's super short
because I am not that
strong

III
I'm rather particular
about my
prose
and my pecs
… could use some work

IV
This is my push up
poem
not much use of
repetition
because my biceps
aren't built that way

V
I really do prefer
sex as a way
to work
out

VI
I'm hoping
to build up to
better poetry

VII
One push at a time

the sex sort of sucked

[4/27/01 @ 11:48am]

she didn't know how to
touch
and I didn't know
how to
tell
her
that I had fallen
far enough
not to care

instead,
I would whisper nothings
that were
more than less
into her
ear

I would touch,
tease,
taste
till she could
come
no closer

I had fallen
far enough
not to notice
that she came
and then went ❦

She won't be writing about me

[12/07/98 @ 1:30pm]

She won't be writing a poem about me
… so I guess I'll have to write about her

I'll make it totally fantastical,
hot and steamy,
certainly sexy,
yet still sweet & safe

Our hands will hold,
our holds will hug,
our hugs will bring us home,
while our touches will taste of tomorrow

… whatever that means!?
… but it does alliterate
… and this is supposed to be a poemy thing

I'll enthusiastically endeavor in inventing silly new clichés
to overindulge her in
I'll *write* that she misses me… a lot!

… hey, it's possible… someday

Fiction is truer that fact
if you feel it enough, see it enough,
dream it enough
… and get it published

She won't write a poem
about that time,
you know that time,
the time we
walked waywardly on West End Ave.,
when we talked totally tangentially

She won't write a poem about that time
we kissed caringly
and sipped champagne
between the rails of Track 29
in Grand Central Station
then we jumped aside
and we laughed
and we laughed

Damn it. It's not true.
None of it. I have no details.
She won't write a poem about all those
things we never tried to do.

Damn it, I wish I had a better
imagination

… to remember those times when…

Now I remember!
… that time we…
… no I don't

This needs a rewrite
… no *she* needs a rewrite!

She has poetry
… he has none
… it'll never work
… can't you see?

If a picture paints a thousand words,
it only means I have no photographs
to present to you as proof

She'll write a poem about *him*!!

"Nah, nah, nah, nah, nah"

Please block out her
passionate poisonous poems with your
hands over your ears
… just like she has blocked out my
heart
… my hope for happiness
… *our* halted hope

When she serenades *him*
with sacrilegious sentiments
won't you please put your
hands over ears chant *"Nah, nah, nah,*
nah, nah… We can't hear you!"
Instead, listen to the poem she has the
potential to write about *us.*

It's all wrong… her and him
Her and *me… that's* right… can't you
see?
… there would be so much poetry for
us to write about.

I loved her first
I have first dibs
… really!

She won't be writing a poem about me
… and all those times
… we never shared
… we never did. ❦

Simple Math

[02/04/98 @ 11:08pm]

Beautiful math teacher approaches.
She likes my stuff.
I like hers.
Math teacher says I peaked inside her head.

"Why do all romantics get dumped?" she says.
"Good question," I think.
"Would you dump me before we even began?" I think.
"Would you dine with me?" I think.
"Can I be your suitor?"
All unsaid.
I connect with her right away.
I know this.
"Could we be a couple?"
"Could we give it a try?"

"May I be presumptuous enough to ask your phone number?" she asks.
"Was that a sign?" I think.
"Is that my cue?" I cluelessly consider.
Bad with picking up signals I am.
I need to count on the math teacher to prove that our one plus one can equal two. ❦

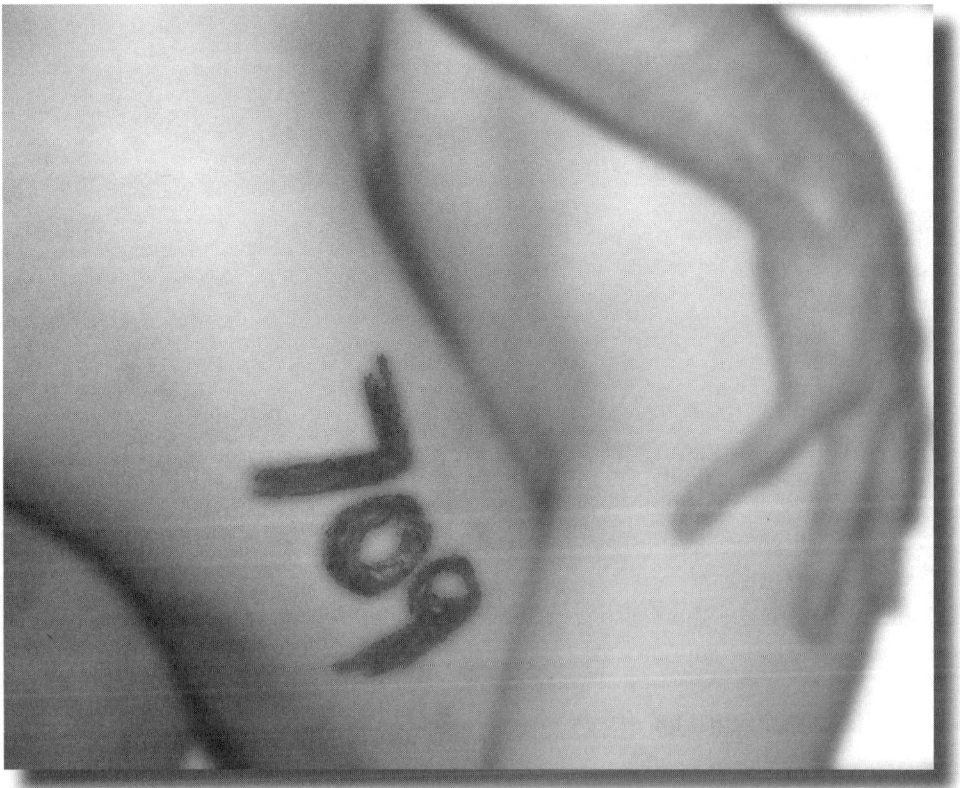

7:09am
[she dreams a dance]

[01/17/02 @ 9:45am]

7:09am

tick

She dreams a dance

Tucked under covers
she clings till alarm rings
in somewhere between
one to one hundred
minutes more

Her lover left
this morning
to do this or that,
balancing futures his specialty,
while she slips across her past

He wants to marry her
while she wants to slip some more
because she is not yet done daydreaming

She trips now instead of dipping
and the dream is fading
and the clock still ticks
too slowly
one more tick
one more tick

Her lover left this morning
to do this or that,
something important to everyone
or no one,
certainly not her

Moments before she showcases her beguiling style,
dips while she dances in dream,
slides her knee between an old lover's legs to
see if she can still trust his affections

While wary of Irish girls who daydream daily,
her dream lover dances close
with a passion more purposeless
than the this or that she now knows in a responsible romance

He burrows knee
between her thighs,
makes her squirm in her sleep

He engages her in a dance not quite
clean cut enough for the man she now forgets in her night,

Passion used to be her purpose,
her style, her spirit,
before she compromised on something less
than the everything she needs
a compromise from something that sizzled
to something than doesn't even quite simmer

But it's safe,
he's safe,
so safe

Concise with poetry,
her spirit knows no such disciplines

This was before she settled for something simpler
something with a sense of sadness,
masked in a make believe
that simple and safe sells better

It sells better to the business plan she made in high school
for how a picture perfect life is painted
and what adults do
when they act like adults

But still she dances
she dances in the dark while
little more than half alone
and dreams
and dreams
and dances just a little bit more before she wakes

She keeps herself warm
knowing she is still loved

She doesn't believe it's a smart thing
to learn to tell time
when there are still things to be done before dawn

The clock ticks and she clings to the covers
for just a few minutes more

tick

7:10am ❦

simple sunset
[07/25/02 @ 9:00pm]

I
Sailing around the city
on a corporate cruiser
bought by the graces of
mass merchandising
I simplify things
slip into the sunset
ignore them all
(they all seem to aggravate
me anyway)
and study the sun being secreted
behind West End buildings
in a *hide and go seek* shuffle, of sorts

II
The DJ, probably as a joke,
plays "*Sailing*" by Christopher Cross

I am growing to like the sound

On my third free beer
(I won't count the four Heinekens
before these Coronas)
I'm beginning to ponder the *pour* fate
of all the limes sacrificed
to college coeds and
post lay-off certified CPAs
who are tired of peeling labels
off other branded beer bottles
to make this or that
wish come true

Lime tastes better
and helps put a bite on
the aftertaste

I was never good at getting the labels
off anyway,
and don't know what to wish for
after a successful peel

III
I simplify things
and slip into to the sunset

I wish my lover were here
to be satisfied by something so simple
it defies the decadence of a corporate
cruiser
overloaded with foo-foo cocktails,
drunk sales reps,
and a waiter
who won't stop making passes at me

The sunset has made me happy
but I'm still not gay
"*not that there is anything
wrong with that*"
it's just that my girlfriend
prefers me my way
and would enjoy this escapade
and a kiss with the wind
between our lips
and the lingering light
of a sun now set
somewhere behind New Jersey ❦

black and white
[10/04/02 11am idea]

This poem cannot be written in
black and white
it needs a
color space to invade

I need to make u
squint your way through
a spectrum [of syllables]
of wonderfully written words

This poem cannot be
read
in a monotone
it needs to find
more frequencies
to fill

It needs to make
your ears bleed
red from recognition

This poem cannot be
printed
on any paper
it needs to feel more
substantial
and touch you
in your most pulpy place

This poem cannot be read by you
today
I need to give you more time
to acclimate
to these surroundings

This poem is not ready
to be written,

It suffers
from premature birth

It is colored
stillborn
in black
and
white ❦

PRE
MATURE
POEM
HERE

a poem too sappy to index is below
[5/18/97 @ 9:55pm]

Show me the magic
inside my heart

Show me the place
where lovers meet

Show me the music
that connects souls
and my feet will follow
inside her footsteps

Show me the moonlight
that will be my guide. ❦

I think I'll have a drink now

[08/05/02 @ 4:09pm]

I can sleep late
dream another dream

like that one last week
where I imagined
waking up
mattered for much

I think I'll have a drink now
maybe two or three

till I forget work tomorrow

Do you really think
anyone will notice?

I'll let Peter get the last cup of coffee
And Sue *something-or-another* can bring
the donuts

Will "Will" whats-his-name,
that boss guy,
even notice if
I don't show?

I think I'll have
a drink now
and sing myself a lullaby
right here in my chair

Staring at the wall
I start to see spots

[sip]

tiny spots

[sip, sip]

so many spots

I can sleep late now ❦

Less than more

[10/20/02 8:20pm]

More than less
I make her cry
by standing here
and saying what I say;
doing what I do

Less and less
I *make* myself care
that we lose each other
more and more
as we turn
each perforated page

In each written word
I find new ways to
tighten screws that
screw us both
to the walls of our backgrounds
and force us further and farther
into our own recessed cavities

And in each silence
she states so clearly
how she suffers
from all the subtext
we have yet to scratch

It's almost deception the things
we don't dare declare

like about my father
who I forgot too fully
and too fast;
faster than her fears of falling out of love
faster than I have fully fallen in

If I said I love you would I suffer
more than less?

More and more
we understand each other
less and less ❦

A poem for player poets and their pray

Girlfriend, I am not a
player
it's just
the poets that perform here
make you think so

social serenades are what I
do
and sometimes it seems
I do unsettle some
women;
make them shuffle in their seats

and, it is totally true,
that sometimes they may
indulge themselves
with initiatives to initiate
a conversation
or maybe even something kind of carnal

I have the backbone of a
beatnik, beat down by too many of
his own verses
but I know
I would never
let one of them
compromise
my
"artistic"
integrity

no matter how tempting
the taste of their teasing tequila
come-on might be

Come on,
baby,
don't you know me
better?

And what was it you
once said to me
to make me care enough
to consider kissing you
behind the bar?

Can't you see
I wasn't seriously
serious about that big
breasted babe
you caught me with
in a tongue twister
tonight?

You straightened my syntax out
and this could clearly
never happen again

You are my poem now
so, if for no other reason
than that,
shouldn't you
realize in
each
line
break
that
I am not a
player
I am
just a poet
that aims
to please
all his
patrons ❦

Oompa-Loompa, I love you
[10/08/02 10pm]

Oompa-Loompa doompady do

Honey, I'm s-so s-sorry about last night

it-it won't happen a-g-gain

I'll t-try to do b-better

Honey, I love you
I do, I do.

I've got another riddle for you.

Honey,
I'll start to t-take out the t-trash?

And I really do like your creamed c-corn dish

Honey, sh-should I pick up the g-groceries on my way home?

You can live in happiness too

I can get that socket switch too for your c-closet

And wasn't I supposed to patch up the pa-patio in the back?

I'll get the grouting stuff from the garage

If you learn to live like the umpa, dumpity do.

Honey, didn't you w-want me t-to take the k-kids to the movies
so you can rest
how about I do that?

And the grocery sh-shopping too
why don't you just take a little nap

l-l-leave it all to m-me

Oompa-Loompa doompady do ❦

consolidating china

[sometime in September 2002]

she will switch to caffeinated
as a compromise
learning to stay up late
discussing dialog
from some Sam Sheppard scene

even the ones
where the dialog is a
bit disgusting
and decadence abounds

I will learn to love
the language of all
her subtexts
as I sink into her hieroglyphics
[and apparently ridiculous riddles]
'cus I care for her
enough to try
reading her right
from the inside
out

she'll try new techniques
of patience to put on
and up with my escapades
of prose and poetry
even when it seems
perfectly perverted

I'll learn to love
bugs or at least not
to scream so much
when she shows me some

but still I will want
to begin with
her birds and bees

she'll spccialize in
straightening my tie
because I have a tendency
to wear myself
crooked

... and her ragged

But I will wash that woman right
into my hair
and let the dandruff decide
that she is so worth the
general grooming

and complete compromises
and the amazingly inane arguments
about fish food and
playboy pornography

Someday soon
I may even be
consolidating china
or, at the very least,
pitching my paper plates ❦

Pez poem [for promotional purposes]

[10/09/02 7pm]

This is my Pez® poem,
a patently preposterous ploy for
commercial endorsement

I aspire one day to become
the Poet Laureate of
sugared Cereals

But, first, my ploy will be for
plenty of Pez

I figure I can call myself
"the *sweetest* poet this side of
Secaucus"

I can dole out decadently delicious
little pieces of colored candy and let
the sugar rush
do most of my work for me

It's cheating with confections,
but
I
clearly
don't care

Maybe one day
Cincinnati based corporate creatives
will snap on their thinking caps
and pop my head back
and put it pedestalled upon
a Pez top

Click back my neck
and pluck out a poem
carefully contained
in tiny tablets
of sugared *something-or-another*

A smile is certainly certain
when something so
staggeringly silly
is at stake

Shouldn't all things in life be
so simple
and so sweet?

Shouldn't all people's problems
be remedied
with tiny pieces
of colored candy?

or some such stuff

Pez anyone? ❦

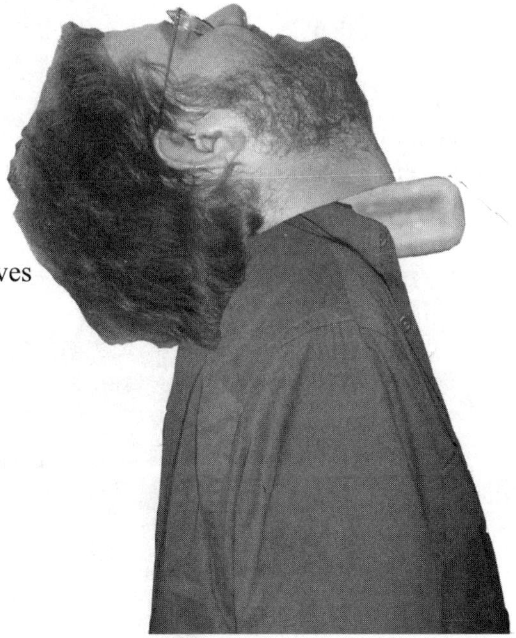

I could fall from here

[10/24/02 9pm]

Sometimes I stand on chairs
and I realize, all too well,
I could fall from here

all 16 inches to the floor

I could fall from here
and stub my toe
on the floorboards of
my own foundational fears
and maybe curse
that I had fallen
so far

But, so far, I have yet to
stand taller than this step stool

I could fall flat on my face
and set myself up
to be speechless

Still, instead, I will be bold
and stand on one leg
because I am just that
dangerous
and in charge
of this conundrum
of standing on stools

in public places
presenting my private
parts

all for your
amusement
and accolades

[At this rate]
soon I can rule
the world

one chair at a time

But, first I need to
start with the basics of balance
and begin
with the constant
challenge of creating courage
by doing something silly
like standing on this chair

I could fall from here
[all the way home] ❦

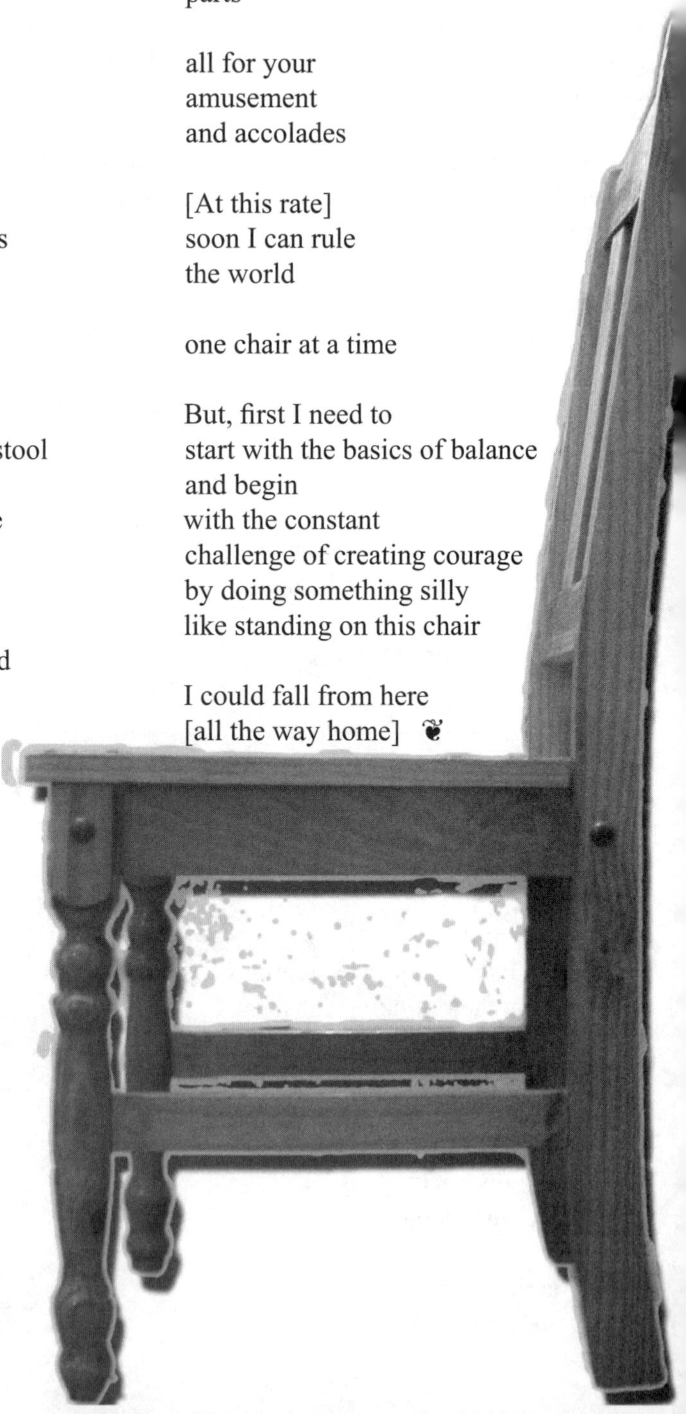

My mailman must know me

10/30/02 3am

I used to think
babies came from breasts
and that big babies came from big
breasted
mommies

I was a 13 pound child
and figured I was
Dolly Parton's kid
until I realized
I simply couldn't
sing

And I used to think
that I was
a special delivery
the mailman made
to my mother
because I just didn't look
anything like my dad
who was so much smarter

I figured I was more parcel post

And since my paternally posing father
claimed to be a Freudian psychoanalyst
I couldn't help but
think that thinking
such things about my
mother and the postman
must be really, really bad

But the facts of life
still confuse me

I am not feeling so smart
and I want very much to crawl back
in my womb
only my mother keeps reminding me
I don't come from
where I think I do
and I am no longer
welcome to visit ❦

when I fall in love

[09/05/02 12:36pm]

i will be fucked.

totally!

I will lose my balance
as I begin to fall
into a place where I care
about being chastised
for stupid things

like stopping the stutter to
speak straight and then
stand straighter
while consistently
caring about
junk like
general grooming

I'll start to clean carefully
and wash
with washcloths
and shell shaped soaps
and be careful about
the status
of things like
toilet seats

I'll try not to spray [too much]

I'll drink beer from a glass,
dispose of my
disposable dishes,
fill the fridge
with FRESH stuff

When I fall in love
I'll be fucked

I'll start to dribble
dialogue,
talk in simple silly
sentences
with SuperSized binges
of baby talk

possibly need diapers
from all the sappy shit
I'll be speaking

I'll get A.D.D.
all over again
and again and again
misbehave
whenever possible

all for the extra attention

When I fall in love

I will be fucked

I'll be on time
to the fucking Figaro *opera*
but late for leaving my lady
each & every morning
talking trash
and taking it out too

I'll be late for work
as a regular thing

and diabolically
distracted
from all the my practical purposes

like my paycheck

When I fall in love
I will be fucked

I'll be duck pin bowling
instead of playing poker, batting balls
and paying bills

I will take pride
in miniature golf score cards,
friggin' floral arrangements,
and care about curtain colors

I'll be broke
from calling card calls and Hallmark idiocies
and financing flowers
on credit cards

Shit I'll even
suffer shopping

I'll be considering centerpieces
and noticing knickknacks,
buying "brick-a-bracks"
and needing riduculous napkin rings
instead of caring about sensible things
like sport's scores
and burgers, beers and big breasted babes

When I fall in love
I'll be fucked,
certainly clueless,
stupendously senseless,
so much so that
I'll get lost all the time
in her smile
and not bother getting directions
to get back
to anywhere but there

When I fall in love
I'll be fucked
silly
and
senseless
and
loving
every
magnificent
minute
of
it

**LOVE
IS A 4
LETR
WORD**

what is it with poets who...

[09/04/02 @ 10:10am]

write poems about poets?

Aren't we commissioned to write
about sunsets [or such]

Why tell tales about Taylor's*
teaching talents
or sing sonnets to Sirowitz* along to
when we can care about something
more bare
and ingratiate our *own* instincts

Marty might not
want to get mixed up
in your papers
and, me personally,
I would never want to
father feelings of ill will
making *any* McConnell* mad

And, since it is still the McCarthy* era,
we should treasure
what JACK has to say.

Let's *read* what he wrote,
and then write something *different;*
find something *personal* to pen

... without the who's who

Stacey Anne* certainly could care
less if you drop her name
she has taken too many to her Chin to
care much about you
she has her own issues, after all

How about YOU
[and me]?

FRANKly speaking,
I should be responsible
for [mis]representing the
the madness [and magnificence]
of my own impoverished
[Mc]Courtships**

Instead of penning a Barb'ed*** poem
about the prose of,
Roger Bonair Agard,*
shouldn't we be
guarding our own gifts,
making it more mainstream
and satisfied studying those sunsets
we let slip by?

Instead of envy (or awe)
towards the gifts
of a certain celebrity
like Saul Williams*
shouldn't we be worried about
whether or not
what we say will survive
the breeding season
of open mike venues?

The classics would certainly
see things different and wouldn't
want you to yawn about Yeats,**
care about Keats**
or bore us all with
your tirade or treatise
to the language of Lord Byron**

Even the lady of the lake
wants more
from you

Certainly the classics should inspire,
but the poetry is in the poem
and the purpose
not the person or the poet
Surely name dropping is not the
dynamic of deed we should decree

nd the baddest, bad-ass Bard,**
'ILL, HIMSELF,
'ould want us to look inward first,
ıen outward
but hardly down the roster
f the open mike

/hat is it with a certainly
lam sensibility
/here decibels are what decide
'hat we do and do not do
. and where names are
/hat go noticed?

)on't we all have a flower to focus on?
. fine female?
/laybe a baby born
f simple sex
/ho just drifted to someplace
n her sleep?

n the night
am sure your little girl
s seeing something simpler,
omething without names

Certainly your newborn is studying a
unset
or such]

n her dreams, she is seeing something
quite *simply*
beautiful

(maybe even you)

Although, I do have to admit I
wouldn't mind it
if Milton** had *sometime* mentioned
ME

.. just in one simple stanza or so ❦

-
* Taylor Mali, Hal Sirowitz, Marty
McConnel, Jack McCarthy, Stacey
Anne Chin, Roger Bonair Agard and
Saul Williams are some *incredibly*
talented performance poets. Don't feel
so bad if you don't know who they are,
but please try to check them out
** shame on you if you are not well
read on these references
*** you *must* hear Roger's Ken &
Barbie poem
**** I yearned to work Yolanda into
this poem, but failed fully

60 second singles

[04/11/02 @ 2:30pm]

Hello, my name is Steven,
a technical talent,
reckless romantic,
and always a friend to any friendly
smile

define yourself in 60 seconds or less

stand tall,
say you are single,
seek to change status

seek to find
same or similar
of obviously opposite sex

seek to cuddle more
than less
and sip champagne on the seashore
or, at least, from an air conditioned room

with a view,
swift room service,
and plenty of pillow mints

seek to hold hands,
kiss caringly,
be seduced into
sizzling sex
then *seriously* snuggle

dance daily,
well, ok, maybe once weekly

seek to spout off
about appreciation of arts,
individualism in the specifics;
preach politics in the abstract;
mention music, minus my collection of silly, sad, and sappy songs by artists that certainly aren't Seal;

coffee best as cappuccinos,
with extra cinnamon
and one of those tasty thin long bisket-ty thing-a-ma-jigs;

At local indie cinema
properly popped popcorn,
hold the grease

but not the constant charming conversation after the credits roll

drive fast
so as to not be late
to kiss slow

[pauses, smiles]
just because
it's better that way

stand tall… don't slouch… speak succinctly
say you are single
seek to change status
in 60 seconds or less ❦

didyaeverhereabout

stolen

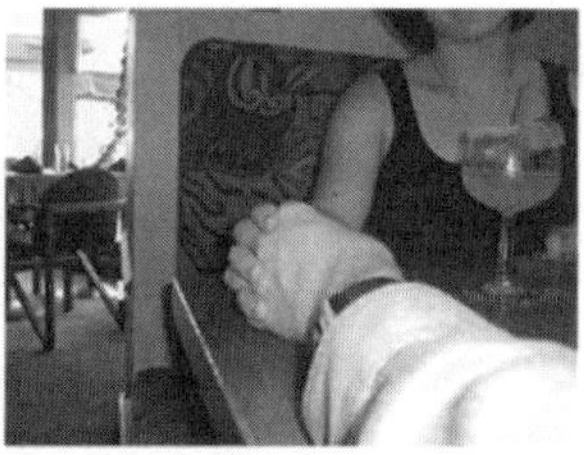

snapshots

stolen snapshots

[7/18/99 @ 6 p.m.]

warm champagne
Charles River
hot, searing August night
glasses empty… lips full

snapshot

secreted sunset
blocked by damn building
warm breeze
kiss to cool off
too hot to do anything but
must control the hands
must slow things down

"we will spend the night, won't we?"
she asks
"you're the boss... seems likely," I say

snapshot

reluctant snapshots
almost avoided
delicious, delirious

carded at Chili's
her 21 to my 34
not Chicago… Cambridge
margaritas with extra salt
stolen kiss over dimly lit table

snapshot
almost avoided… taken

jump forward through sumptuous
sweaty night
… hot night
at dive bar now, it's open late
last call for that margarita with a little
"something extra in it"

wow, what an expression!
"uh, oh spagettios"

captured

15 fingers intertwined in a dance
no snapshot
fingers busy making
love

stranger sounding *way* too much like
Alan Cummings,
our Master of Ceremonies,
stranger to our interlude
but friend to our cause
"that's niiiiiice"… so niiiiiice

snapshot

jump forward
drunken walk
where to? who cares?
no more than 10 steps
broken with a kiss
"Do you dip?" she asks
"Why, of course!"
"I trust you," she says
it's a luscious
back bended kiss
a new pattern

10 steps
stop
kiss
tease
touch
dip
kiss

snapshot

"we will spend the night, won't we?"
you bet

snapshot

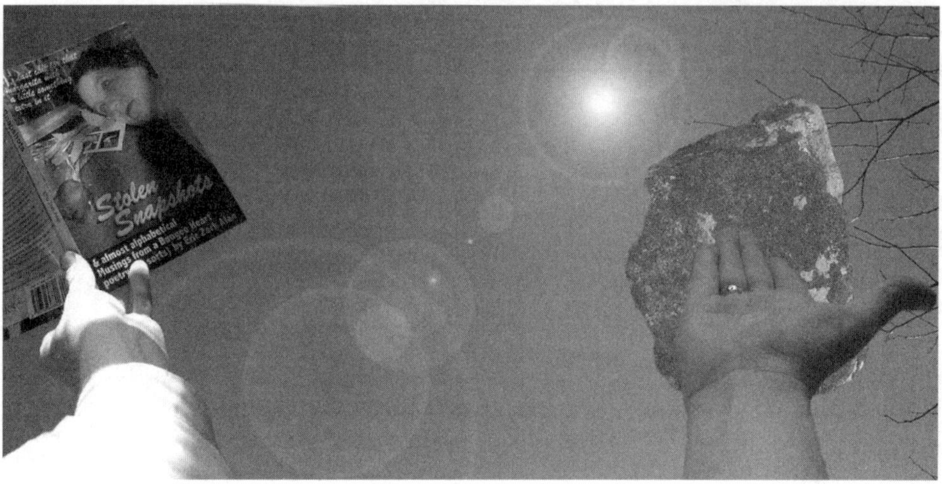

Stone wall

[07/04/01 @ 9:00pm]

You built a fortress
or a front line
I'm not sure which

You stand on one side
duck out of the way
protect yourself
from memories,
PopTart poetry and
Pez dispensers that,
somehow,
promoted passion in small sugar rushes
inside all your outermost pockets

You slip and slide behind the wall,
protect yourself from *my* memories
of how many times
you slipped inside my mouth
while searching for words to declare
your singularity

So you build and hide

I lay down
more out of habit than purpose

I lay and look at where you were,
before you built,
and I live with what you let remain

I can't see above your ridges

Taking a break from frustrations
of constructive silences
I wish you had used brick
instead of stone
as the color would add more poetry
to your absence
and the counting would be easier

counting the moments we made love,
counting the thoughts
of telling you I had fallen,
counting the sting of every salted glass
we sipped from,
and counting the tears,
the tears left after all the counting

Stone by stone, I count

I turn my attention away
and study the sky
I pretend to study the sky

orientation on orientations

I lost my last love
to a
lesbian lover

maybe it was something
I said
that made her switch sides

something like
"I love you"

"I love you
just the way you
are"

I lost my last love
to a
lesbian lover

maybe it was something
she heard
that helped her
have a change of heart

something like a slogan
maybe a military mantra

something like
"be all you can
be"

I lost my last love
to a lesbian lover

maybe it was something else
something like her smile
looking in the opposite direction ❦

Stuck Together

[10/13/97 at 1:45am]

"We are stuck together," she says.

Completely naked
in a bed with reduced afternoon rates
and absolutely stuck together

Her head resting on my chest
legs wrapped over and around mine,
sheets lie half covering us at the end of the bed.

We have formed a human pretzel of sorts
… one of the most comfortable kind.

"Nothing can separate us now," she says. *"It's like that glue."*

Yes, that is exactly how we were
… like Crazy Glue.

[It is 4am. We are in no rush to be anywhere but here.] ❦

How can I
tell him
he no longer
makes me
smile?

Texan Blank

[04/18/98 @ 1:43am]

That cactus above me could be from Texas… my home state
Is that where I belong now?

I really am such a beautiful woman, I am sure you can see that.
But you have to look at the smile I can't wear right now.
Then my beauty would blind you.
I carry my hands flush by my side now… I don't know what to do with them.
If I put them on the table he might want to hold them… and I am not so sure I want that any more.

Why can't he still make me smile? Sometimes he does, but why can't I smile now?

My face is a portrait of a beauty without a landscape to rest in.

If only he could help me find my landscape.
If only he… someone… anyone… could help find my landscape. If only I could find it.

Last month I remember when I rested my head on his shoulder. It just felt so right then. I am not sure if it was his or just any shoulder I needed but it felt so right.

I really did wear a smile then… an ear to ear kind… I am sorry I couldn't have captured that moment in a different photograph to show you.

I eagerly took his hand on that same night. I just didn't want to be without it. His hand had such tenderness and warmth. He really does like me… he really does appreciate how special and unique I am.

It was the first night in a long, long time when I felt like things could change. I have been alone too long.

How I need to be held!

And those kisses, they really were special. He even wrote me a poem or two.

For a few weeks it all seemed to be coming into place… nothing grand… but *something* felt good about it all.

God knows I am not looking for a future here… just a contentment with individual days. Baby steps. So what happened?

Here I sit across from this same man that made me smile and I am paralyzed. What am I afraid of? Am I afraid he will care too much too fast? Am I afraid he's just been a substitute for a peace I need to find within myself?

If only I could smile now. I'm afraid to take another sip of coffee. I really could use one. But what if he tries to take my hand?

How can I tell him he no longer makes me smile? ❦

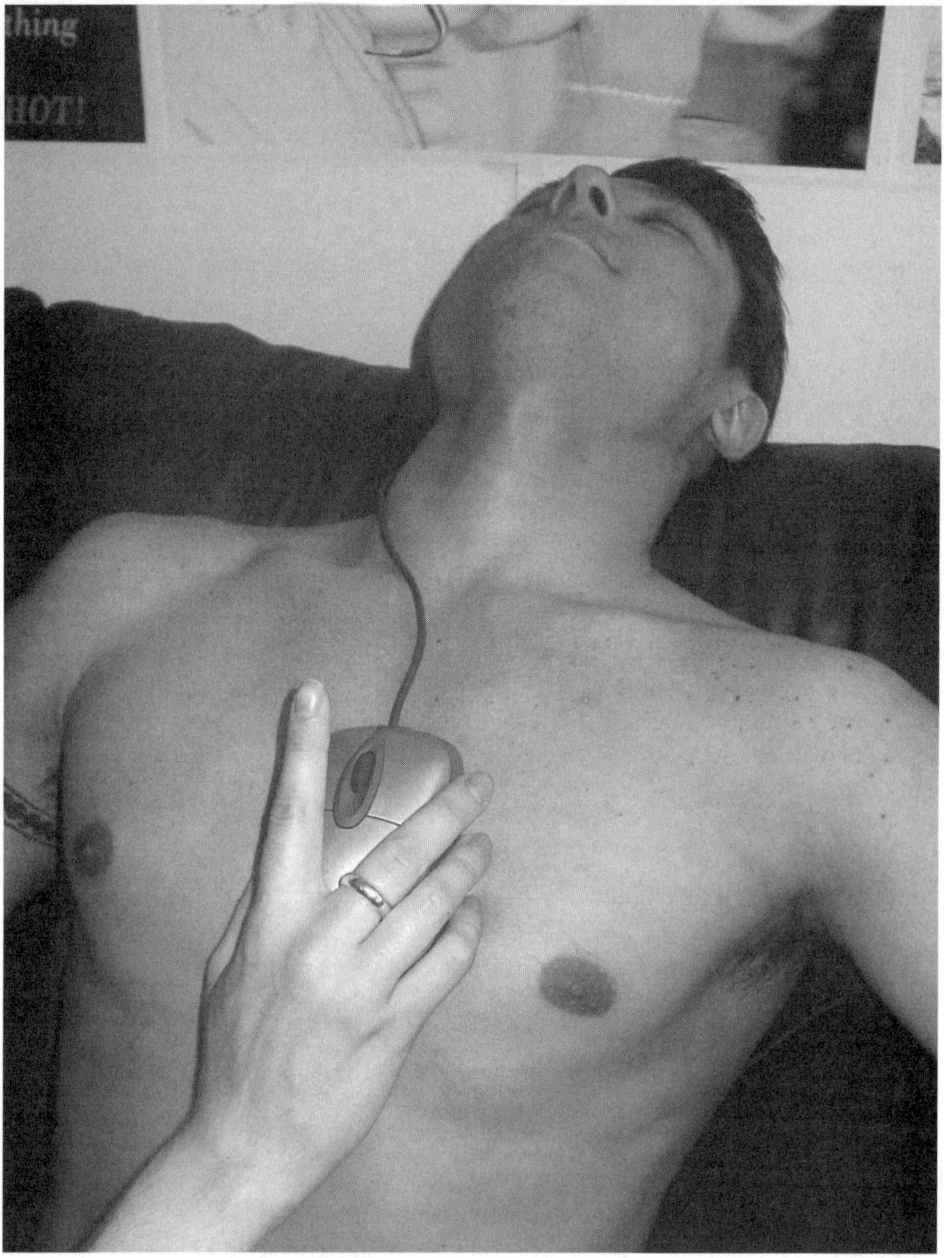
thing
HOT!

The Rhythm Method
[& cyber seductions]
[04/19/2000 @ 9pm]

I: B.4 [play]
finding the rhythm method into your arms through these lines
the rhythm of our remote digital dance
held within the pulse of our removed romance
finding the rhythm to your phosphorous seductions
rhyming in email prose
send [mail]
wait
send [male]
W A I T!
rhythm to me
my rhythm to you
pacing with polished prose
short strokes to careless keys
fighting a frenzy
laptop balanced upon a bulging banter
returning your receipt
[no time, no need to punctuate]
seducing with syllables & half-filled breaths

II: v2.2 deluxe and Y2K enhanced
when at close range we offer a new kind of smiley
lost in this tight rhythm of newfound kisses
no time for breathing at this pace
but who needs the damn air when we share such sensuality
so, so fast, but we are in no race
beat, beat of your closely held heart
caress
time sticks
but our rhythm skips
time will tell truth of lies and lies of truth
time will cool our falsely filled fulfillment
and pause our passions
but right now,
in this rhythm,
kiss after kiss,
we are not done ❦

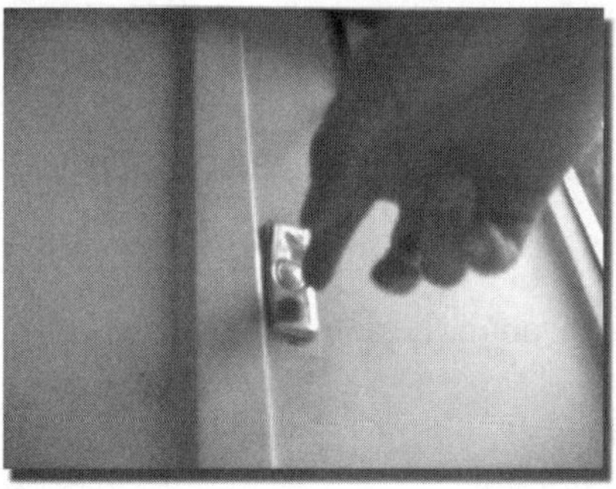

This is my favorite part

[07/28/98 8:50am]

"This is my favorite part," she says.
"Mine too," I think.
Unsaid… until I've had time to practice more.

Jump back.

Six hours ago.
A single red rose in hand.
Ring, ring… no sound. Broken doorbell.
Knock, knock… a bead of sweat on my brow.
Quickly wiped… don't want it to show… must *seem* calm.
She opens the door.
This is the part where I don't kiss her hello.
1st date… too soon for that… we haven't begun yet.
Rose goes into impromptu vase… a glass embossed with a naked man.
Don't ask… I didn't.
As she cooks and we talk… I realize this is my favorite part.

Four hours ago.
A twelve-inch TV serves as the medium of entertainment;
the entertainment that isn't held within my arms.
Say Anything is the movie… but we say nothing.
So soon she is snuggling, leaned back and resting in my arms.

This is my favorite part.
When she leans back into my arms.
She leans forward for a sip of her drink…I gently brush my hand down her back.
Very gently… very innocently.
Scratch that… very suggestively.
And then she falls back into my arms.
You see, it wasn't an accident the first time… it was not a mistake that she was in my arms.

I have an urge to be naughty… 1st date… too soon… let's take it slow.
But there will be no avoiding the sensuality.

The perpetual sense of touch… soft, soft touches.

My favorite part.

I want to get to *know* this lady better
… to see if this can grow.
There is potential here… too soon to tell for sure… but potential.

Two hours ago.
The movie has been over a while now.
It's the bewitching hour… and there is a spell.

The spell that freezes me in place.

I should leave now.
But I don't want to go and I am not being asked
… no hints
… no yawns
We are both tired… but tired in each other arms.
This is my favorite part.
One arm wrapped around her and the other holding her hand.
We are going to stay this way for a while longer… there is no rush.

One minute ago.
"Is this where I kiss you goodnight?"
"If you like," she says.
I like.
I rush in… go too fast.
"Easy, slow down," she says.

First kisses, not a skill.
This all is so new.

"This is my favorite part," she says.
And now I take it slow.
Right now, *right now*, *this* is my new favorite part. ❦

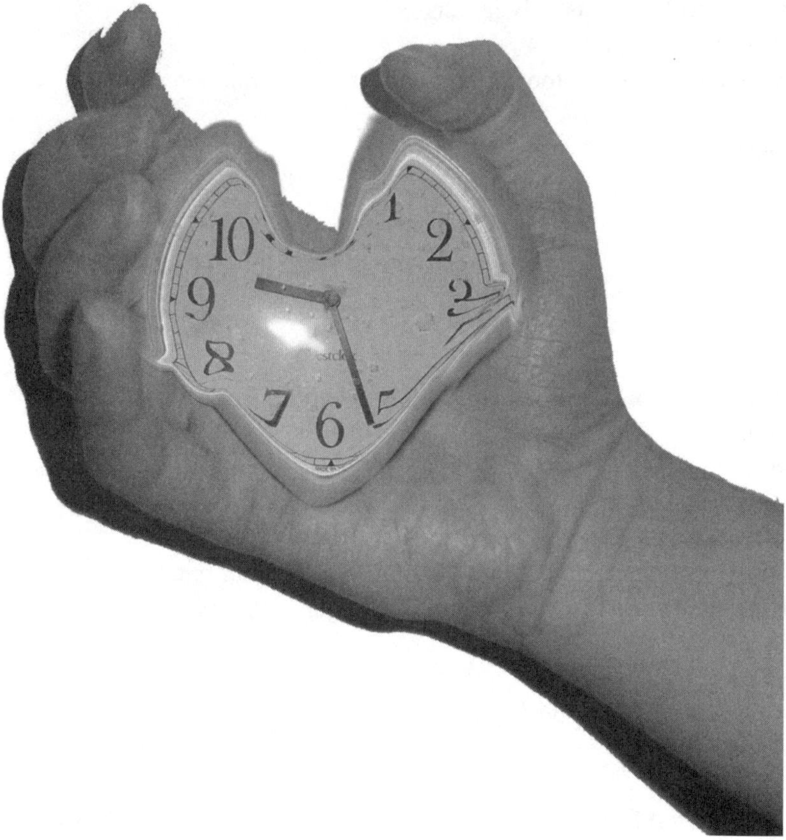

Three Minutes to Your Heart
[November 1998]

[slow]
I have three minutes to grab hold of your heart
to make you see
to take you on a ride… in here *[points to heart]*… and get you back here *[points to floor]*

Three minutes
Tic Toc

[fast]
Three minutes to enter my heart… your heart… our heart
Three minutes to show you my love
her love, your love… who's love?

Three minutes to hold you tight… so tight
say goodbye and let you go.
Three minutes to be your friend… your lover
and then forget what we had… in three minutes
Three minutes to get your attention
keep it
make a point
make you feel
stranger to friend
friend to lover
lover to see ya later… see ya never… but do have a nice life
three minutes
how strange!
Three minutes… tic toc.
I might drop a name or two… stand on a chair or even scream
to get your attention
for my three minutes

"We said Hello, Goodbye"
Phil wrote that line… it got my attention
You see, I just dropped a name… I got Phil tea.
I digress… three minutes
Tic Toc…
Don't want to overstay my welcome.
Don't want to bore you in four.
Life is so fleeting… attention is so fleeting
This is so fleeting… friend… lover

[slow]
Hold on.
Times up.
Hello, goodbye
Don't forget to write

But just for three minutes. ❦

A totally silly, sexist & obviously offensive counting poem

[written in character, of course]
[06/04/02 @ 8:00pm]

1	1 day soon I will take you home
2	2-morrow, maybe 2 see you totally naked

3	3-mendously excited I already am about a ménage a trois with u, me and that delicious dame from the dollar store, Regina. I recount an imagined encounter in my mind again and again 2 many times 2 count
4	4, sometime soon, I will meet you and I *will* indulge you in freaky 4-play My 4-skin has already taken its hat off, stood at attention and smiled 4 u
5	5 dollars is all I have 4 our 1st date Maybe I will treat u 2 *Mickey Dees* 4 dinner & sips from a 6 pack
6	SEX is hardly certain when thrift is telling you that maybe you should be looking *harder* But, then again, you seem a bit 6-ly and like a cheap conquest

7	7teen sex starved singles *have* to have had you by now and it looks like they all seduced you with Happy Meals™ and soda Slurpees™ and, anyhow, didn't you
8	ATE already 2-day … ain't that enough? I don't want u 2 blow-t 2 badly 4
9	to-9-t you will be mine as I in-COUNT-er you in at least 69 ways one of which will certainly be *Suddenly* you spin my way look straight into my eyes, a *fantastic* first and stare deeply and *almost* smile And just as a
10	10-t pops up in my pants you say: *"There ain't no way I'm letting you get to* ***11*** *not now, not never, and certainly* *not with that* *horrendous Happy Meal™ move."* ❦

Happy Endings

[05/09/02 @ 10:45am]

Happy
endings
happen

They
really
do

Within the breath
between this moment
and our next kiss

Now ❦

stolen snapshots
presents
Beer
Things to
do with
beer bottles
by Eric Zork Alan

Shameless plug:

Buy "*Stolen Snapshots: Things to do with beer bottles*" in 6 packs or by the case from www.stolensnapshots.com. Singles available from Amazon.com, etc.

The book is loaded with much silly stuff such as seriously stupid drinking games, beer gardens, beer bowling, beer trivia and *really* bad pickup lines, etc.

The book is best read after the first [or second] six pack of beer is consumed. I promise you it is less funny when sober. Mr. Alan wrote it when he was a bit tipsy, it is best read that way.

things to do with beer bottles

[07/29/02 @ 8:14pm]

first

launch the lime down her neck

force finger down shaft

tip her upside down

and poke it in hard

swirl it around

swing upright

and swig

take a second and

appreciate her taste

now that you have her attention

it is time to be more creative

and show her

the 69 nine other things you can do

with beer bottles ❦

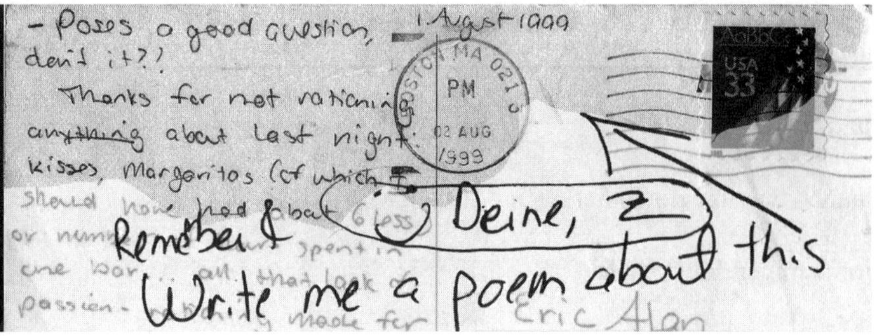

Under a circle of tears [a.k.a. "a poem that is true shite"]

[01/28/2000 @ 9:40am]

[Editors' note: we *think* this piece is *intentionally* rambling with mixed muddled metaphors and an overall lack of poetic conciseness. Poets, go figure!?]

Under the incredible illumination of a circular sun I found love, skating.

Under the umbrella of too many years and tears I found waiting,
then found you.

Under the pastel circle of the moon,
i trapped you for the moment.

You trapped me better.

With the patience of Job & curse of Kirk
Like a bad suit of seventies sorrow
i wear the wrath of your psychedelic Kubla Khan of caustic caring,
beaten by the tides of your whimsy, suffered with my bad metaphors.
Sucked out to your "see ya later;"
smashed back to no one's shore.

Bloody on the rocks I still pant from teasing tastes of your past passions.

With a trace and taste of your lips I still see your moonlight
and wait to curse my new dawn.

I am only a man filled with painful poetic clichés and, all too real, tears.

I have lost my poetry.

And there is no love lost,
but poetic promises of potential
to bind to daydreams that linger long past sunset.

That is until I read the poetry you refused to write.

Did you write a poem for me?
Would you? Can you?
Can you remember enough to invent me memories of when you painted your thoughts in different patterns?

It was an August night… it was your place and your Champagne was warm, your passion hotter.

Under the moon we were trapped trying to make more than 10 steps
without a dip, a kiss, and a dance.

We were trapped under that moon.

"This is all too sappy, I am all too sappy," I say,
aware of your romantically challenged disposition.
under the moon, while seduced by our sunrise, and so out of character,
you repeat for the nth time
"please, do go on... don't stop, please don't stop."

We danced in every place,
within every glance
and within every touch
we kissed in between and within each line we spoke,
losing rhythm of dialog, never caring to keep the tempo in tune
with our lullaby; the lullaby of each look,
the looks we used to interrupt our sentences and thoughts.
We never let the moments go by without our "niiice" touch of grace
and we never thought of tomorrows.

We know all too well that is *always* a mistake.
making plans, we knew, was always a mistake,
while making kisses and making love was never wrong when trapped under *our* moon… the one you misplaced in our afternoon sky.

Too glad & afraid you called in a new day.
A new day with no sap and a forgotten taste of longing.
And WE were so drawn to that mindless, senseless sap.

Under a circle of questions and tears,
I am left with no more kisses and fast fading memories.

In the here and now, you are ice cold and a distant twin to yourself
with an opposite spirit and absolutely no poetry to share.

All beauty broken, firmly flushed; finally,
as if the bedroom mirror were not your friend,
and, as if, you didn't already prove yourself lucky & blessed
with the beauty of beginnings all around.

Afraid to *relax* and *feel* just a little bit frightened
by what just might be *our* moonlit magic
you dare to skip dessert and skip away.
As if we hadn't already played out that sad scene of sudden stopping.

Caring is not a weapon wielded by lovers, it is a blessing,
and that ought to be your most constant concern.

Passionate properties fraught you with fear of finding something
or nothing.

But it is all the same when you just don't try to try
to fall inside the orbit of my arms
and hear what I am saying. I'm saying:
"I need to see your insides. I need to find your fears so I can betray them with a friendship that may grow to be love once you let me inside."

"I know where your mystery began. I'd like to show it an end."

Recurringly, I tell myself to forget letting you find me,
again and again.

And I fail.

Spinning in circles, I suffer the gravity of your apprehensions
to hold on just long enough till you learn to hold on.

I forget our dance.

What were our steps? Was it 10 and then the dip and then the kiss?

Or did the kiss come first?

There is no love lost, love takes so much *more* time to tell
and so much *less* fear to find. [don't fight]

I am stuck.

Fatally flawed by passion, romance and remembrance,
I am trapped by so many questions unanswered.

No, not fate, I am trapped in the selfless sacrifice of missed kisses.
here and now, my thoughts damn thoughts of tomorrows.

I want nothing more than an endless *present* succession of first kisses.

And, as I try to fill this with wit, I realize you never found your sense of humor
and you lost your sense of self.

Under a circle of some undiscovered metaphor,
I am stuck with a poor poem trying to call you back for a simple kiss,
one with promises of no tomorrows,
with promises of no promises.
A simple kiss just for the taste of it in this breath until the clocks melt our moments into something much more meaningful.
You lost our chronology and skipped past the beat of our romantic rhythm
when you made plans to run away from any plans.

You made God laugh.

Why did you do that when you know all too well that's a bad joke?

With bad metaphors and rambling poems, smothered under a circular stream of recollected kisses, I am trapped in the prison of my memory; and in that funny sound you make.

Will you make that sound just once more… and fill me with a better poem? ❦

[Wake me] 1:40am

[09/23/99 @ 1:40am and May 2001]

When you are still wet from the rain inside
wake me with the taste of Tabasco truths,
and a telling theology
its gospel silently sung in tender touches

Wake me from our closed church of caring

Wake me with a whispered seduction in broad daylight

Wake me with a sip of Champagne from a two dollar glass,
with a cold plate of stolen French fries,
your kiss trying to find the other side of my smile

Wake me with a mis-understanding of basic math
1+1 = 1

Wake me with that smile you have worn too many times to outgrow

With salted lips and a midnight collect call

Wake me with breath in my ear

Let me eavesdrop on your fantasies
and argue with your fears
of finding beginnings with boyfriends

Wake me with whispered memories
of the river, the sunset
& sated carnal sunrises
seduced by silent surrender
to your simpler sins to dine, drink, dance and
make believe when you make love

Wake me without a reason

Wake me in a sinful way

Sing to me like you *say* you sing in the shower
stay sexy and show me
as I take the detachment in hand
make believe we are lost naked
in a surprise rainstorm
while the heavens come from all around

As we lose control
let us dare the drops to dance with us
as you sing
as you sing

Wake me,
wake me with a kiss
that doesn't dare care why ❦

the way u make me steal

[07/31/01 @ 2:40pm]

[*with MAJOR LEAGUE* apologies to: Aerosmith, Bee Gees, Billy Joel, Brian McKnight, Bruce Beresford, Brian Adams, Dianna Ross and ALL Supremes, Davy Jones & all his cohorts, even the WhiteOut guy, Eric Clapton, Huey Lewis, Jacksons [all of them, even Michael], James Taylor, Janis Joplin, John Denver, Ken Russell, Lionel Richie, Meatloaf, Porky the Pig, Pointer Sisters, The Princely guy with no name, Robin Williams, Sammy Hagar, Sly & all his Stone Family, Spike Lee, Sting, SuperTramp, Talking Heads, The Beatles, The Troggs, Tom Waits, Van Halen, Van Morrison, Yvonne Elliman, etc.]

You've got those lemon drop
*martini eyes**
and other things that make me steal
lines to learn to love you by.

If *Time Waits** for no one
I'll still croon for you *Jersey Girl**
after all

*The way you make me feel**
fuels me with *Pep-*

See my arsonous desires
to light fires in our hair & under our table cloth
as we sit down to *dance, dance, dance**
*to the music**

*Hey, hey** you make me feel funky
Please can't we *Monkee around**?

You have made me a *Day Dream Believer** and
with you, *I can never get enough**

*You've got the moves to move me**
and with *the way you make me feel**
it's no wonder I steal

It's no wonder that you make me *Bad** & *Dangerous**
and you are so much *more than a woman to me**

I am filled with your *Night Fever**
*If I can't have you,** I am merely *staying alive. staying alive**
*ah, ah, ah**

It is a *Tragedy!**

[You are my siren and you make me steal]

Stolen Snapshots*
are only the beginnings [of my larceny]

*Every time I see your smiling face**
I know although *I've seen fire and I've seen rain,**
there just *ain't no mountain high enough**

Every McKnight I kneel down and say
*you're the only one for me**
but STILL,* *do you miss me, anytime**?

Sometimes your Head Talks to me in my sleep
this ain't no *love during wartime,** yet
you *burnt down my house**
long ago
*q'uest que c'est**
with that u
*wild thing**

But where else am I to live?

Because, in my *traveling prayers,** I know
*you're my home**

We sip red & white tears from our tales in our *little Italian restaurants**

Car, *VAN** or performance poem
even in HALE[n]
*i can't drive fifty-five**
when I *run, run away**
from my *crimes of your heart**
I must *jump,**
jump away

You certainly STING my sensibilities
But *STILL**
*Be still my beating heart**

*I'm just so excited**
I need to spring*[steen] *two steps forward**

to take *one step back**
into your totally torrential *tunnel of love**

Hot damn, *baby doll,**
U R ROBIN me of my WILL[iams]
and *I'm on fire**

You make me steal;
tramp *my way** into this SUPER *crime of the century**

I confess, I confess
You're *bloody well right, bloody well right*
*got a bloody right to say** that
My crime is to care 2
*hold your hand, yeah, yeah, yeah**
to care 2 cuddle
and to need to steal moments to
have some [More-of-some] u &
*make love to you in the afternoon**

And in the autumn, as I leave
I fall to my feet
realize you fill me with *crazy love**

My emotions have fallen like *dominos** from a *caravan**
straight *into your mystic**
*moondance**

Maybe I would miss you less
in *Margaritaville**
But only *maybe your right, maybe I'm crazy**

But certainly *STILL,* I think I love you**
and I am lost nowhere near *Albuquerque**
but still *I wanna go home**
with you

While you lay down, *Laaaayla,**
*sunshine rolls over your shoulders**

In your *rocky mountains, I do get high**
As you *come down, down on me,** I scream
TAKE ME HOME,
take me home to your country roads.

*I do sooo love your mountains, momma!!!!**

Then *take me home** , turn me out like a light &
*strike a pose**
then *dress me up in your love**

Take me out to *celebrate,** let's call it a *holiday**
Goddamn, just *like a virile virgin**
*u touched me for the very first time**
making me *crazy 4 you**
and *the ways you make me steal**
ways to woo you
with rhythms of romance
and *ridiculous* performance poems

*I don't want a new drug,**
I want you back*
Simple as ABC, I want you back**
You and me,* much much better than *Bobby McGee**.
*Hot Patootie, bless my soul I really love the way you rock my roll**

You've got those lemon
*drop martini eyes**
and other things that make me steal
lines 2 learn to love you *buy* ❦

basically Budweiser

I'm a Budweiser kind of guy
I like to keep my beer bingeing
simple
and sip from brown bottles

none of these excessively indulgent
and incredibly expensive
imported brands

I like Bud; it's kind of cheap
but still tastes terrific
in a mild mannered sort
of way

Like with sex
I like to keep it simple;
basically
missionary
is my method;
I don't have the time, talent and patience
to practice many more techniques

I stick
to Coca Cola;
the cans are still
kind of cool
and it's not so
sweet as to be
saccharine

When driving home,
it's a Honda
because
I'm not driving when
I'm horny so I don't need
no sexy sports sedan
to pick up chicks

Basically, I'm a Budweiser
kind of a guy
I like to keep things simple;
life seems to sell itself better
that way

and I could always use
a nice cold can of beer to set my sights stra

SEX
is
Good
Beer
is
Better

When I met you

[07/13/98 @ 1am]

We haven't kissed… we haven't touched… not yet.
But we will.
When Harry met Sally.
When I met you.
It's on the TV… a 12-inch color set from the turn of the century.
It might as well be black and white… it's on the set right now.

We haven't touched… we haven't kisses… not yet

But we will.

You sit back on the couch
… next to me
… so close.

The side of my arm gently slides against your side.

It's not deliberate… not a motion… not a move… it's just where you ended up.

I savor the teasing touch.

Your blouse is a soft textured fabric. Is it cotton? I don't know… I don't care.
I don't remember the color… I don't care.

I remember the sensation of touch.
… the very first between you and me.

Harry and Sally… they sparked… and so do we.

We will touch… we will kiss.
But not tonight… I don't think tonight.

That final scene… when Harry kisses Sally
… when I WILL kiss you.

It's midnight… the movie ends.

When Harry met Sally… and I met you.

We haven't kissed… we haven't touched… not yet
But we will. ❦

Wordless Poem

[11/06/98 8:55am]

If I had a girlfriend, I wouldn't need a poem
to wrap myself in and around and through.

Adjectives, adverbs, metaphors… phooey!
Words are no substitutes for holds.
Romantic rituals are natural rhymes.

If I had a girlfriend,
I wouldn't need to speak,
I wouldn't need to learn to write… to spell
… and formatting the printed page for *performance* poetry is such a bitch.

If I had a girlfriend,
I wouldn't need to stand here, talk here, cry here.

If I had a girlfriend,
I wouldn't need a poem.

I like you guys and all
but you kind of ruin the wordless intimacy of the moment
… that is meant to be here between her and me
Me and who?

I normally wouldn't bring a date here
the words would only distract from *our* poetry.

Lengthy, lascivious, longing… wordy, whining, wanting
OR
Having… holding… home
…
Let me see, I think I can answer this one. Just give me a minute.

I wish I could ask you all to go home
… all but my nameless, faceless one.

Dammit, will you please introduce yourself!
So we can get on with OUR poetry.

Unrequited love
…
"Stop writing about unrequited love," they say
Well, that one is easy…
REQUITE IT!

If I had a girlfriend, I wouldn't need a poem
to wrap myself in
… and around… and through. ❦

Remembering the man I never got to know

[6/6/97 at 6:07pm]

"Mom, what's wrong. Where are you going?"
I was five and I was following my mom down the hall.
She did not answer. She kept on walking.
I don't remember what time it was.
I don't remember what woke me.
But I remember following my mother… trying to get her attention.
I follow her down the stairs.
"Mom, what's wrong?" I ask again.
Again I get no answer.
She opens the door leading down the stairs to the garage entrance.
And, this I remember, she tells me to stay at the top of the stairs.
She did not explain why.
She slips out of view as she enters the garage.
I don't remember what our garage looked like, but I know that is where she went.
A moment later she returns and collapses in tears at the bottom of the stairs.
"What's wrong, mom?," I asked.
But I am sure I already knew.
I had lost my father.
Dead of a heart attack, in the garage I don't remember, at the age of 43.

That's my memory of my father. That's all I have.
I seem to remember that morning so well.
I may remember none of it.
It may be my memory of telling this story so many times.
But it is all I have.
I can't tell you if I loved my father… although I am sure I did, I can't remember it.
I can't tell you if he loved me… although I am sure he did, I can't remember it.

Later I would see him lying still in a casket. This I remember.
I remember visiting a tombstone… a small flat one… inconspicuous.
It was a plaque with his name on it.
I imagine my mother placed flowers on it, but that I don't remember.

He would come to me in dreams for a few years, but I don't recall a message.
I don't remember his voice, his demeanor, his habits or his smile. ❦

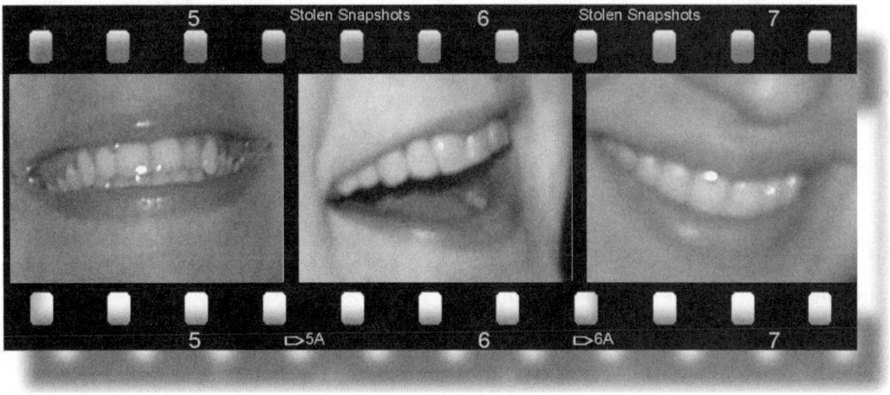

She smiles

[6/7/97 @ 2:40am]

She looks at me and gives me that smile.
That special look and special smile.
It is meant for only me.
I am not a selfish man, but I would not share it with a single other soul.
The smile keeps me warm, memories of it fuel my day.
When I am away from her I just imagine its glow.
I have made this lady smile and she does this when she thinks of me.
My, how special that makes me feel.
It is only me that can put her in this state. She thinks of me when apart and she waits for our reunion at the end of the day. She waits for that embrace that immediately follows the smile.
She looks forward to our midday call. And she smiles.
I can't see it… but I know she wears it.
When we are separated she becomes distracted by my absence.
She needs my voice, my touch. And she waits to see my smile.
I feel so special. This all makes me feel so special.
I belong here in her look.

I don't yet have the name or recognize the face that wears my smile… the smile meant just for me.
I haven't yet figured out where to go to find it.
But when I do I will know it… and I will be home.
I don't know if happily ever after will lie in this look.
I don't know how long it will last. I believe in fairy tales but know we don't always get to live them.
But we can appreciate the moments. We can learn to appreciate the special connections and the sense of belonging.
I belong in someone's smile and I will find the face.
Yes, and then I will be home. ❦

Palm Pilot™ poem v 2.3 B4

[11/27/02 @ 7:30pm]

This is my palm pilot poem
filled with
short sentences
and no stanza breaks
just great
*[excuse me as I scroll down,
down]*
just great mispeled sensibilities
and a lithium based love
of our language

It is short, sweet and
only sometimes
*[excuse me as I scroll down,
down]*
only sometimes spel cheked

conveniently I
can flip and find this
poem because
I am comfortable
with it's tactile touch

I am not the kind of guy
to get caught
between the sheets
*[excuse me as I scroll down,
down]*
between the sheets of a
handwritten poem

It's a nerdy need
that brings me here tonight
in super small type,
from an 8 bit, backlit
[excuse me as I scroll down,
down]
backlit love for linguistics

I know I turn you
on so much
[tap tap]
so much
you try so desperately
to find my switch,
some switch,
any switch
to turn me
*[excuse me as I scroll down,
down]*
to turn me
off

But I am not afraid
to show you my
*[excuse me as I scroll down,
down]*
show you my hardware
and strut my software
and swing about my
extended stylus
in the name of acclimating
you to my
[down] [down]
to my art

I do know
I am the best poet here
[excuse me as I scroll down,
down]
the best poet here,
here behind the mike
*[excuse me as I scroll down,
down]*
here behind the mike
right now,
right now,
with a palm pilot
and a poem

As I scroll
line by line
head in hand
I am guaranteed to look like a
*[excuse me as I scroll down,
down]*
look like a geek

This poem is guaranteed to
get all the girls
*[excuse me as I scroll down,
down]*
to get all the girls
to get as far away from
me as possible

But then again can
I be bothered with them
anyway
when my head is in my
hand and Tetris is still just a
tap, tap
away

Hey, I know I am
*[excuse me as I scroll down,
down]*
I am not much of a poet
or performer
but at least I can say
I can afford
to PENtificate to you
in public

Would you like to play
*[excuse me as I scroll down,
down]*
play with my Palm-a-Sutra

I am not ashamed to
play with it in public

*[excuse me as I scroll down,
down]* ❦

Truly, madly, deeply

[1/8/98 @ 11:56pm**]

Truly, madly, deeply… I remember
Song on thc radio makes it impossible to forget
I can't release you from my mind
You keep coming back

I want to finally forget
easing days from longing
and nights from despair
song on the radio makes me remember
something about a "juke"
and that Chicago song I had never heard before

Truly, madly, deeply… I remember

I remember that first night in your bed
high school naughty; aunt down the hall and silent muffled discretion
your eyes closed, I just enjoyed the texture of your jeans
as I touched you through and through

Lionel Ritchie makes me remember a silent drive

So many songs make me remember our car seat boogie
and that we never picked "our song"

Truly, madly, deeply… I remember ❦

God is like a girlfriend, a really, really great girlfriend

[10/25/02 9am]

I've always been an agnostic
choosing not to choose and not
be connived into having faith
in something as fantastical
as all that is told to us by
Times Square theologians

but still I am not beyond the sentiment
and not beyond
wanting a little loving
and daily doses of
hand holding and
and certain sense of harmony

because I do get lost waking up
in an ocean of empty sheets
and I do fear falling
asleep when not dreaming
of being a spoon in God's soup
or at least being spooned by someone
special till I slip into
a deep, deep slumber

God is like a great girlfriend
a really, really, great girlfriend
the kind you would sing songs
for on Sunday morns
and morning day nights

"I've just called to say
I love you"

Like God, great girlfriends
are well endowed with
enriched wonders
and feed milk to the masses
making us come back
for more and more
with unwiped lips
and lots of love in return

Like God, great girlfriends
are wise in ways
us guys can never really
understand

and I'll be damned if I ever understand
what makes them so darn
temperamental
like tornados
on a mission
to humble our hormones
whenever we misbehave

A great girlfriend, like God, is
fierce in a fight
and always, always right

but the making up part is always so, so
satisfying
that we are never left
without a certain sense of gratitude
at the greatness
they can sometimes give
even when under pressure
and a bit disappointed how
we don't always deliver
what we promise
and we rarely live up to their
exceedingly high expectations

I don't need God now
I just need a girlfriend
a really, really, great girlfriend
who I won't fear to have faith in

faith that she will still stay
even through the strife, sorrow
and slip ups
and fill me with foundation
and with a future
full of amazing "Amens"

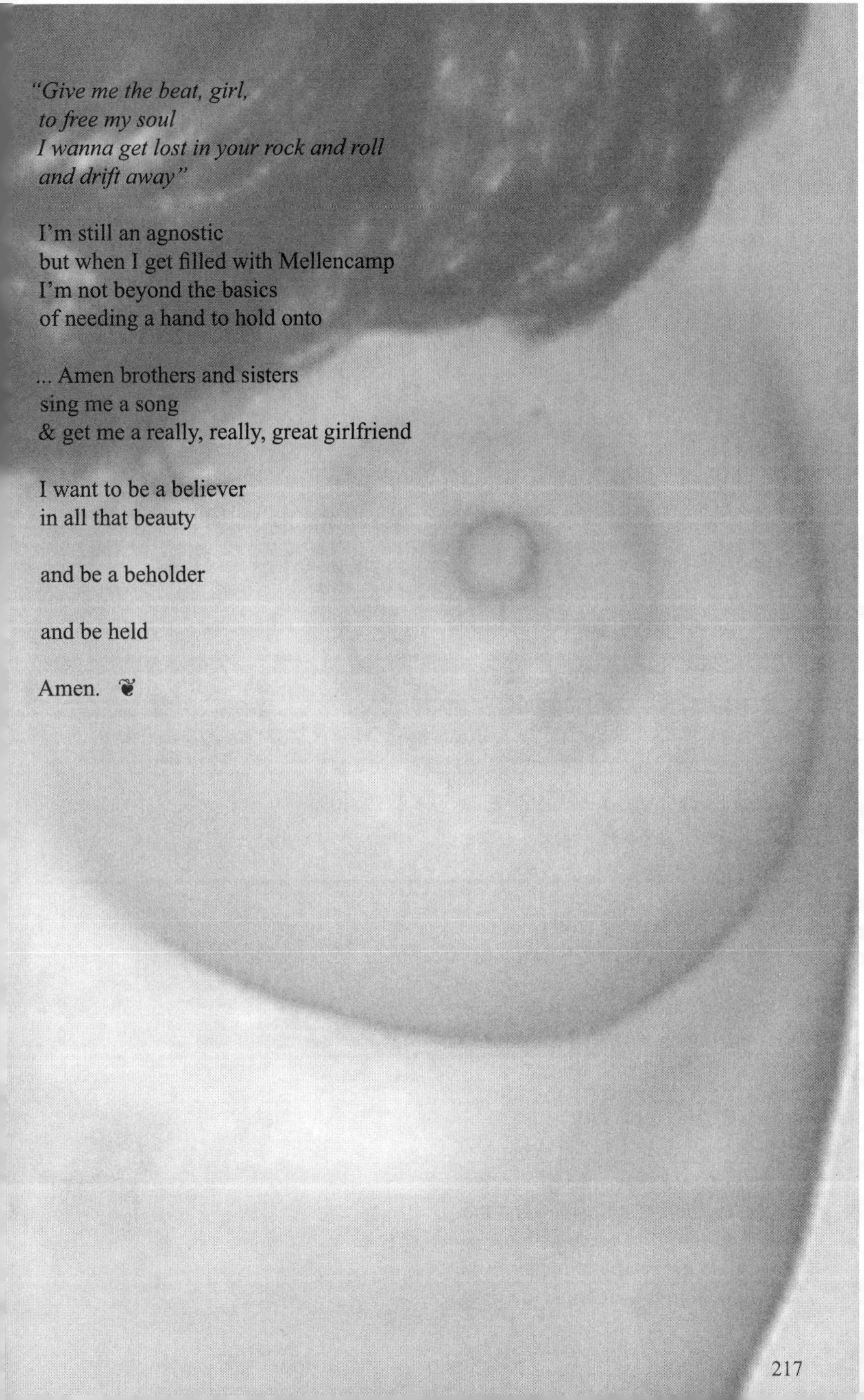

"Give me the beat, girl,
to free my soul
I wanna get lost in your rock and roll
and drift away"

I'm still an agnostic
but when I get filled with Mellencamp
I'm not beyond the basics
of needing a hand to hold onto

... Amen brothers and sisters
sing me a song
& get me a really, really, great girlfriend

I want to be a believer
in all that beauty

and be a beholder

and be held

Amen. ❦

You know I was so drunk [Good night kiss]

[09/09/98 @ 8:50am]

2:31a.m. taxi waiting with no place to go
I was so drunk I kissed you at your door.

I was so drunk I asked you to dance
we took the floor, shared a groove, our groove.
It just felt so right.
"ABC... 123... baby, you and me, girl!"

I was so drunk I forgot the odds.

So drunk I forgot it was you and me.

So drunk I got totally trapped in your eyes
and fell flat into your arms.

You know I was so drunk I talked to you about leaping buildings in single bounds
… as if we could
… just like we did.

I was so drunk I did not camouflage my caring.

So drunk I might have actually danced well.

So drunk we shared a *European* kiss
more than I asked,
more than I ever hoped.

So drunk I came back to your lips for some more.
2:31 a.m.: taxi waiting with absolutely no place to go.
You know I was so drunk I was delighted to miss my train and catch your lips.

Here's to alcohol, to tipsy dancing, to holding your hand.

Here's to flash photos while I cop a feel here and there.

Here's to a drunken hello.

Here's to you and your charm,
to you and your beauty,
your tilted smile
and that spirit that draws me in so close.

Here's to a first kiss way too late,
but totally on time.

Here's to the hope that there will be another.

[You know, *we* were so drunk that we kissed
goodnight.] ❦

ABCs

[05/30/2000 @ 3:40am]

Anytime, always
anxious and awaiting
always amorphous
amorous and angry

Broken beauty breathes & berates
berates big beauty
bore…
babe, babying…
"boy, oh, big boy" to *"bye bye"*

Catch caution
catlike
caustic
corked, coked
cost is costly
caring is covert

Dance dangerously
dance dark and dim
do but don't dare dare
don't hope
don't help
don't dance dopey to dope
dance till dusk
dance to dark
don't, don't, don't

Everything, elastically even
eventually evoking ecstasy
even evoking emotion
evoiding eric, edward, everybody

Flirt first
fake first
flake first
Faust forgave
forgive family first
forgive friends forever

Girl gets guy
girl gives [good]
girl grits,
girl gets gone
goodnight
goodbye
gone

Hope holds happiness
hope holds home
how?
how!

Impress
imagine
implore
ignore

Open MIC

Megan Buckley

Literary Agent, author
Age: 25
Favorite poet: Frank O'Hara
First Poem: age 5 or 6
Poem subject: the ocean

Bar

Inside, before five,
old men already argue
over empty glasses
and ashtrays spilling
with cigar nubs
and cigarette stubs,
crumbling like lungs.
One tippling liver
plugs a finger into
the shoulder of another,
who rebuts with a shrug.
They keep good company
thus, seated and warm,
between sips and drags,
away from the pace
of the streets,
the strange Asian flavors,
and the pimples of spittle
on the sidewalks. ❦

You should write about this

[03/18/98 @ 1:40pm]

Moments before it was a mad rush to the train.
St. Patty's Day, 1998… the 11:58 train to Tarrytown.

She is too tired… too drunk… and she needs a place to rest.

She finds my shoulder and rests.

We both need to be held.

I want to wrap my arm around her.

I fear disturbing her sleep.

But she needs to be held… and I need to hold.

Each moment is filled with a peace knowing she is comfortably resting on me and the frustration of wanting to offer her more comfort
… of wanting to bring her further inside.

Could I be a part of her dream?

If I could hold her more completely could I enter her dream?

The conductor comes to collect. I pay our fare.

I overcome moments of hesitation and fear and slide my left arm around her.

She is still asleep… never disturbed.

I gently caress her arm… each finger with a separate task.

Every moment while she slept I was wide-awake.

We will never kiss again. ❦

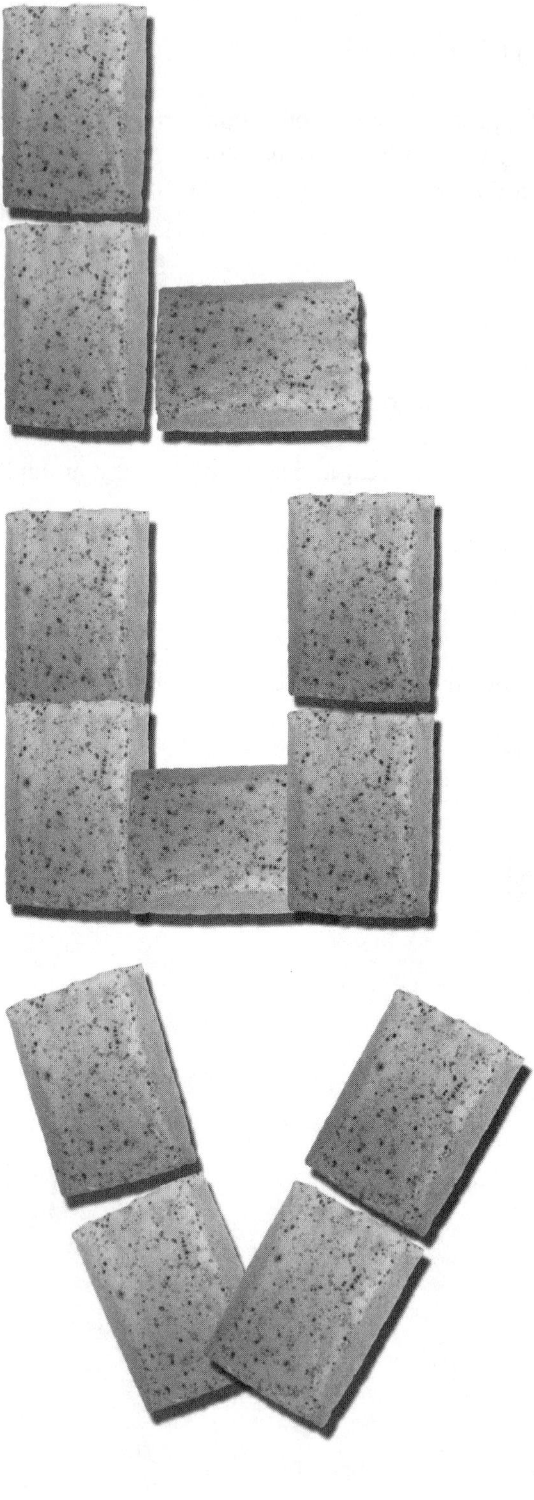

Zork's Pop-Tarts: Strawberry Sprinkled Heart

[08/21/98 @ 9:30am]

7:30 pm: one toaster oven purchased… a needed prop. My heart demands it.

3 am: one dozen boxes of strawberry Pop-Tarts, the sprinkled kind, are distributed in a pattern on her desk in a small cubicle… they express for me in glucose and berries what I can't say out loud.

And you can't cover someone's desk with Pop-Tarts without providing a toasting method so there goes the brand new toaster oven.

She's got great breasts… but that's not what got my attention. No, it was three dates before I even noticed them. No, I'm not blind… but something in her eyes enchanted me.

And the words she said… just to me… and the voice that brought those words closer to my ears… no my heart. They had me distracted… my eyes never had a chance to wander.

One day, after our third date, a co-worker says, *"My she's got great honkers."*

I have some crude friends… but I still like them.

"Huh?" I said… *"Excuse me!"*

"You DID notice?" he asks.

I don't answer… silence of the lambs… no, silence of my mouth… sounds of silence… no, just silence. I don't want to sound like a geek. Three dates and I didn't notice.

I reply, *"That's H. you're talking about. Don't talk that way about her."*

Next time I saw her I noticed… nice indeed.

Oh, I would like to squeeze, to lick… just to gaze at their naked wonder.

Stop that. Stop this train of thought. I can't objectify. I don't want her that way.

Yes, I do, *of course* I do! Of course, *anyone* would.

But that's not the point. The point is I didn't notice till after the third date. She had already burrowed a place for herself in my heart… and it never had anything to do with her breasts, or her body, or her beautiful face.

But her smile, when we talked and we connected and I was locked, locked in her eyes, then she had no form to lust after but a spirit and a soul that just wouldn't let me go, doesn't let me go, will never let me go. I am trapped always in her spirit that never leaves me no matter where she goes.

She is so far away now. She is with another man now.

Five dates, that's all we had before we became "friends."

I hate that word… it has four letters we all know.

But I love her, I love having her as a friend, I will take whatever she has to offer.

You see we never kissed. Imagine that, we never kissed. Five dates and we never kissed.

I never tried. I was too trapped in her eyes to even see her lips.

Scratch that. At the end of every evening I tried… in thought, I tried.
But in action never.

That I regret. You know she *might* have kissed me. Who knows she might have.

I never held her hand… if I tried, she *might* have done that too.

Such a wimp I am… but I was too trapped in her eyes and too afraid to leave them… their warmth, their home.

The *good-byes* each night were tough… how they lingered. We took so long to say goodnight. Sitting in the car just being comfortable with each other.

She loves me but not in *that* way. Someday she'll miss me and the holds we never shared.

Her loss, her loss... not her fault.

She can't help it… the way she feels… neither can I.

But I'll still love her… forever and ever and beyond.

It's unconditional.

It's all the more real and true when it stays with me even when she can't return it. When I can't hold her to renew its strength and it stays with me. Wow, it is so strong! I love her so much.

Remind me not to cry now… I think I want to cry now.

But I'm a big boy… I won't cry now. I won't.

I'll wait till later when none of you are around.

I'll put on one of those songs… you know from the tapes I made for her… and then the tears will flow like rivers.

Gee, she even made me use a metaphor there. I *hate* metaphors… they just aren't real enough. Words just aren't *real* enough. You'll have to step inside my heart to understand.

But I'll play the music and I'll cry then.

But they're a good thing… the tears… they remind me about love… it's a magical thing… the good and the bad of it. All amazing emotions wrapped up in one great trick. But it's no illusion, this magic is real.

Hell, maybe she'll even change her mind someday. I doubt it… but I can dream.

Right now, I am stuck in a memory of strawberry sprinkled Pop-Tarts.

She likes them a lot and now so do I. In memory, I am covering her desk in a small cubicle with 144 Pop-Tarts. I am writing a message from my heart to hers.

She's my best friend. I will take what I can get.

Look at all these Pop-Tarts. ❦

Let me taste your tears

[05/22/01 @ 2:10am]

Let me taste your tears
then tell me the truth
about fears and fantasies
of when and where you found a smile in my morning.

In bed, your touch seems too tender to be telling tales.

Let me taste your joy, your rapture and your release.

You read to me of poetic conversations with the sun
and poets who suffered death by dune buggy
and the tragedy makes me laugh.

And, in his poetry and our dialog, you make me believe that we have some verse
and more than just our vice.

In bed, despite passionate pleading, I stop.

With the taste of you still fresh in my mouth,
I have questions and can't tease you till you tell me something new,
something that has been untold till now to friends and lovers.

So I stop.

Being an old fashioned man, I can't come inside
till you let me in where your romantic reservations reside
and introduce me to your deepest fear of finding something in my arms,
something more or less than you long for.
And, here, let me privately peek at the greatest gift of
shared souls just starting out.

So I stop.

This will be my first time
to fall in love with you
and your pain and conflict
of confused cautions.

So I stop.

And I can't yet fulfill your thirst until you make me believe
in your daydreams to edit poetry
starting with one about us,
and about firsts,
and about settling down long enough to find our questions
… and start to answer them in shorthand.

So I stop.

"Will you be back?" I ask.

In a passionate dilemma, you say,
"of course, of course, baby, of course,
but, please, let's not wait till I return when I am right here
... and ready."

We never make love, but we make believe and I believe we can transform sex
into something like song if we just take the time and concern to practice enough.

Let me taste your truths.

I believe we will become good lovers,

rising above the fear of simple secrets that suffer in our bed
if only you stop the clocks
and start to see that we spoon together really well,
and the silences are so sweet,
and we blanket each other so well,
and the stereo sounds so good,
and we don't even need the sex to have the synchronicity.

In 101 tunes on custom CDs
I never made… and never sent
I cry for you in tracks and tears of Van Morrison and Pablo Cruise.

You make me believe that if I can learn to love you,
I can write a poem that would be good enough for you to remember,
good enough to read to roommates.

I want to wrap you in my words
and spell things out for you using only simple emotions and strong sensations.

Let me taste your suffering
and find new places inside your folds to sooth you.

As I suffer for your recollection,
your romance,
and your romantic respect,
I remember I made you cry once while sick at a local pub.

Afterwards, you kissed me deeper than you ever dared before
and told me you would try to try.

In a tearful embrace,
missing your beer and drunk from cough medication
and delusions of false footsteps,
you kissed me deep,
told me you'd try,

and you stopped. ❦

Scene: Teacher Test

[02/06/98]

[Editor's Note: While still sometimes sappy, Mr. Alan no longer lives with his mommy.]

Man:

OK. Before I ask you out I must reveal a few potentially embarrassing details that could disqualify me from dating you. I love Lionel Richie music… the early Commodores stuff, that is. I saw Barry Manilow in concert as a child and Mac Davis twice… but, otherwise, I *hate* country music. I *still* love the Partridge Family because I believe if you ever truly love something you must always be loyal to that feeling. And, of course, I wanted to grow up to be David Cassidy.

It is rare that a day goes by that I don't spill coffee on myself.

I am likely the world's worst dresser and have no clue how colors coordinate.

I really can't spell without a spell checker and I have no clue where just about any country is except that I *think* South America is below us and Canada above… I think.

… and *[with a mumble]* I still live at home.

Lady:

What was that last one?

Man:

I still live at home… with my mom. You know, it's like an Italian thing. I have these Italian surrogate dads and if I were truly Italian leaving home wouldn't be an option until I got married.

Since I am still struggling through the dating phase I'm not shopping for furniture just yet.

Lady:

Well, I lived at home for a few years after college so I guess I can forgive… but the Barry Manilow thing, that I may have to think about for a while.

I'm OK with the Commodores and Partridge Family, but only because it's cool to be retro in the 90's.

And I'm OK with the coffee stains too. Personally, I'm used to hot chocolate stains.

So is it my turn for pre-date confessions now?

Man:

Yep, I guess it would only be fair.

Lady:

Let's see. I have the hot chocolate stains. I have a philosophy against the Internet. I've always hated party lines and the Internet just seems to be one big party line with about 1 gazillion callers. And those UUURRRRLLL things are just way too difficult to type.

I have a really loud laugh and sometimes use it without discretion… and think Keanu Reeves can act.

And I often forget to put the lid back on the toothpaste… and I snore… but don't expect to be able to confirm these two things anytime soon.

Well, that's all I can think of right now.

Man:

All good information. I'll have to explain this whole Web thing to you. It's not nearly as wicked as you worry. All computers aren't evil. HAL in *2001* seemed to give a bunch of them a bad rep.

Lady:

O.K.

Man:

O.K.

Lady:

So…

Man:

So…

Lady:

So…

Man:

So what? Did I forget something?

Lady:

Isn't now when you were going to ask me out?

Man:

Oh yeah, I almost forgot. Actually, I just got petrified for a minute. You know that male preoccupation with fear of rejection and how it affects one's self image and masculinity.

Lady:

Can't say I've ever had fears about my masculinity… you know, being a woman and all.

Well…

Man:

OK. Here it goes [clears his throat]. Now that you know all my obvious quirks, odd tastes and weaknesses would you like to go out on one of those classical boy/girl kind of date things? You know, where I pick you up at seven or seven-thirty and drive us to a restaurant… hold open all the doors and stuff and we eat and then go to a movie. Followed by some post movie coffee somewhere where we can talk.

The movie is fundamental to the first date request… if our conversation falters the movie will always give us a bunch of launching boards for the inevitable awkward pauses. Or the parts where I just don't have an interesting thought in my head.

During the evening I will restrain all my natural male impulses to grope you.

Lady:

Well *secondly*, I don't think you would ever be short of dialogue the way you can ramble on.

And, firstly, I would be delighted to try all the stuff you just mentioned.

I reserve the right to initiate groping if I feel like it. Women's prerogative, ya know?

Man:

I think this is where I try to act calm and say something calmly casual while inside screaming *"Wow!!!! She said 'yes'"* But since I am an honest guy, I'll just tell you I am very glad and inside I'm saying *"Wow! She said 'yes.'"*

Lady:

Well, it may be premature for *that* kind of enthusiasm but at least you're proving you are not like other guys.

Man:

What guys?

Lady:
The *other* guys.

Man:
Oh. Well, I can pretty much guarantee you that. Hey, and don't worry I don't try to kiss on the first date. So I am warning you in advance that if you want to avoid contact with my lips then you should start coming up with a list of excuses for avoiding a second date... because I will be going in for the kiss then.

Lady:
Duly noted. But what if I want to kiss you on the first date?

Man:
Then maybe I should come up with some excuses too?

Lady:
I *always* get what I want.

Man:
Duly noted.

[silence]

Well, I'm out of original and witty things to say for now so I think I better leave you now while I try to collect a few more clever comments before our first date. I certainly don't want to wear out my welcome *before* our first date.

Lady:
You are odd... cute and clever... but very odd. Well, aren't you forgetting something else???

Man:
I don't think so... like what?

Lady:
Like maybe asking for my name and phone number? And maybe telling me a date, time and place? All of these things might help us out a bit... you know with getting together for this whole first date thing and all.

Man:
Well, uh, you do have a point there. ❦

I don't want to read a poem tonight

because my inkwell
has run dry

I already got the girl
(or, at very least, *a girl*
who, at the very least, is pretty great)

[I like to keep silent
when I slip her inside me]

I don't want to read no poem tonight
because I can't possibly
memorize this sentence of sentiment

I already got the girl
(or, at very least, *a girl*
who, at the very least, is pretty great)

So, tonight, I am not here
to play you with prose

I just want to sit back
and listen
and fill myself up with
you

I don't want to read no poem tonight
I don't have the energy
to stand up
and speak out loud

and I already got my girl,
a girl, a great, great girl

I don't want to read no poem tonight
I don't dare take the time
to rhyme
'cuz I just don't got no good reason
anymore

and I already got my girl,
a girl, a great, great girl

I don't want to read
no poem tonight
because I don't feel like repeating
myself from parcels
of print

Read me off the page, if you will,
as long as you turn me carefully
with a tender touch
but I can't repeat myself
stanza, after
senseless
stanza

Tonight I don't have the gift of gab
and I already got my girl,
a girl, a great girl

I don't want to read
no poem tonight
but please do go on
I am here to close
my eyes
and take you in
take you in
like a song
straight
from my lover's lips

so please,
do go on.

-- thanks for YOUR poetry
-- Eric Zork Alan

The End

(or the beginning?
When you decide which, write me a poem of love lost or love found. Or a tale of a niiiice plate of french fries. Write to poetry@stolensnapshots.com)

For the *Stolen Snapshots: Open Mic* **poem of the day** go to
www.stolensnapshots.com

FINAL filler quotes:

"Thank you for having the good sense not to say that *to me!"*

"I've had a really tough day... but I think I would need a few violins to tell you the whole story."

"Sappy is much better than melodrama. It's the same thing without the pretension and a happy ending to boot. It's a win-win situation."

Final wisdom from Kurt Vonnegut, Jr.: "so it goes & hi-de-ho"

Final answer from Douglas Adams: 42

What is the proper question now?

OK. I am done now, it is *your* turn… send me a poem *now* to submit@stolensnapshots.com or go to www.stolensnapshots.com and click on the SUBMIT link. I showed you mine, isn't it about time you showed me yours?

stolen snapshots
presents
Things to
do with
beer bottles
by Eric Zork Alan

How stupid can 1 book be?

It only takes $4 (and a shameless lack of self respect) to find out. This stupendously stupid book may have taken only a quarter of a brain to write, but it is also only a quarter as much to buy [that leaves more money for beer] and where else can you find books available by the six-pack and the case? If you know someone particularly dumb or drunk then this makes a great gift item. In my case, I often like to pretend I am dumb and then I find this really funny. Where else can you find the following highly illustrated stupidity (and all for $4 or less).

- Beer Baths and why they help more than hair
- Beer breakfast/ good for low-fat diets
- REALLY bad pickup lines that will get you slapped
- retorts to really bad pickup lines
- "99 bottles of beer"...the origin is NOT in this book
- How to get free beers in Irish bars
  [untested & probably untrue techniques]
- Drunken beer poems
  [but not too many...don't want to bore beer drinkers]
- all in all, 64 pages of stupendous stupidity for sale for $4 [or less in 6 packs and cases... see order form on back]

PRE- VIEW
OF
"Stolen Snapshots:
Things to do with Beer
Bottles"
[this is NOT a book of poetry...
its a book of stupid stuff]

Beer Bath

Historically speaking, beer has long been known to be good as a shampoo supplement to create a shiny head of hair.

So, if you want to be super sexy, be good to your WHOLE body with a beer bath. While a bit costly, every once in a while you should spoil yourself.

For those special dates try an imported beer bath... after you have been going steady you can switch to PBR.

Type of Beer	$/Gallon	Total $
Imported	$15	$380
American	$10	$220
P.B.R.	$6	$110

*cost presuming 22 gallon bath.
Add approx. 25% for average Jacuzzi.

How stupid can one book be?
See
"Stolen Snapshots: Things to do with Beer Bottles"

Burroughs' Beer

William Burroughs, author of "Naked Lunch", may have been an influential writer, but he had a tendency to work under the influence of substances far more serious that bottled beer.

Sometimes for fun he would test his marksmanship by doing a "William Tell Act" under the influcence of various substances.

But, in 1951 after killing his wife Joan by trying to shoot a highball glass off her head at a 6' range , he probably regretted that he didn't use a beer bottle instead which would have been taller.

Wil iam was in Mexico City where shooting glasses off heads is less illegal than in the United States and only consutitutes a $2,312 fine and about $2k in legal fees. DO NOT try this at home or at your local pub. It won't be funny.

BUYBOOKSBUYBOOKSBUYBOOK

How to BUY some STOLEN Snapshots

*[otherwise known as the ****__SUBLIMINAL__*** ***SUGGESTIVE SELL PAGE*** where author reminds you (and* ***INVISIBLY*** *suggests) what a great gift item these books are and how starving poets appreciate your patronage... please don't make me beg]*

First, call your local book store and ask them for it.
And, if at first that fails, then:

BUY BOOKS

WEB ORDERS: www.stolensnapshots.com
[or www.amazon.com & www.bn.com]

EMAIL ORDERS: bookorders@stolensnapshots.com

PHONE ORDERS: see website or email for more details

BUY BOOKS

POSTAL ORDERS:

Name: ____________________

Organization: ____________________

Address: ____________________

City, State, ZIP ____________________

myrentisdue

Phone: ____________________

didmyelectric
justgetshutoff?

Email: ____________________

Enclose check for appropriate amount and noted shipping for the following:
____ copies of *"Stolen Snapshots: I am not a poet"* @ $16.00 each
____ copies of *"Stolen Snapshots: outSPOKEN" CD* @ $10.00 each
____ copies of *"Stolen Snapshots: Things to do with beer bottles"* @ $4 each
____ 11*17" Stolen Snapshots POSTERS @ $2 each [see poster @ website]
____ 6 pack of *"Things to do with Beer Bottles"* @ $15
____ cases [48 books] of *"Things to do with Beer Bottles"* @ $96
[add $3 for shipping for under 7 books and $8 for case of beer books]

BUY BOOKS

Mail order to:
Alliterative Authors Press
21 Branch Brook Rd. / Suite 609
White Plains, NY 10605

I'm kind of hungr

Even more stolen book blurbs

[This is where the author continues to have people say really good things about him. This is in case you didn't look at the back of the book or flipped past the first blurb pages. Mr. Alan has huge insecurity issues and needs to validate himself through the kudos of others... or, at least, that is what his mother, girlfriend, and therapist think.]

"To see Zork perform in person is to watch the great Viking physically and verbally imbue his work with the emotion and depth of thought with which it was written. Even without that experience (and man, what an experience it can be), the writings, in and of themselves, are a daring sensory blend that tread the line between poetry, essay, and a small town in Maryland."

- *"Big Dave" Mattey [actor]*
- *Star: Toxic Avenger Part IV: Citizen Toxie [Troma Films, NYC]*

"Zork's *Snapshots* are internal word polaroids of ourselves at our best, most awkward, most honest moments. They are the photographs we hide (after we get them developed) for fear they don't show people our best side. In his collection, Zork empties his drawers and invites us to pick out frames for his portraits."

- *Dot Antoniades [poet, actress]*
- *former host NuYorican Poets Café Slam Series*
- *1997 NuYorican National Slam Team member*

"Fascinating book. Zork's mind flows in all different directions. Kind of like a money shot at the end of an adult movie. I highly recommend it (this book... not the money shot!)"

- *Ron Jeremy [actor]*
- *co-star: Killing Zoe and other films*

"Mr. Zork has one of the most original poetic voices I know. A sort of madman with words, his poetry reads like a runaway train, and I want to know the destination, I cannot jump off though I find myself feeling anxious at times, I need to know where he is taking me. You will not read a more original collection or poetry, I highly recommend it."

- *Anonymous reader review from amazon.com*

"Selling nonfiction is a challenge, fiction is tougher and poetry is the greatest challenge of all. Poets need all the marketing advise they can find."

- *Dan Poynter [author/publishing expert]*
- *The Self-Publishing Manual*
- *[Please note that Mr. Alan made you flip to this page of the book looking for the matching blurb from the Poynter poem [p. 74]. Dan probably would approve of any technique to cause a reader to open and then flip to find. And, you see, it worked]*

"*Stolen Snapshots* is what happens when the music stops and you're alone with someone you love."

- *Hal Sirowitz [Poet Laureate of Queens, New York]*
- *Author: Mother Said*

"The first time I saw Eric 'Zork' Alan in action at a poetry reading, I was speechless. Six and a half feet tall, battered raincoat flapping, red hair askew, waving a hand in the air, his other hand holding a visual aid, he certainly had the attention of the audience. Since that moment, I've loved seeing him read in public. Whether he's standing on a chair at the podium or throwing PopTarts to the masses, this guy forces us to take notice, reminding us poetry is, finally, about humanity--raw, real, and otherwise."

- *Ron Egatz [poet, writer]*
- *winner: Glimmer Train & Greenburgh Poetry Awards; Pushcart Prize nominee*

"A six-foot poet who stands on a rickety folding chair to read has a perspective that defies imminent collapse. Like Kudzu, he has an endearing persistence. There's only one Zork. Don't drink the cool-aid, wallow in the alliteration."

- *Mar Walker [poet & noted incompetent low-brow know-nothing]*

"*Stolen Snapshots* is an ecumenical portrait of a zorkist as a young man. Zork takes the loftiness out of poetry, making it accessible to the human heart. He dares to be foolish and have some fun, taking us along for the ride. But don't be fooled–beneath all the zaniness is a sensitive man not afraid to put his heart on the line."

- *Ellen Wilder [drama critic/journalist]*
- *The Stamford Advocate*

"Very rarely do works of art cause me to draw back both my upper and lower lips, but, my god man, Zork has done it. For the first time a poem ['*Things to do with beer bottles*' p. 196] has graced me with a thrill of revulsion. Nice job!"

- *Mike Robin [Dramaturg, Westside Theater/writer]*
- *co-author: "The Osbournes" [Andrews McMeel Publishing] & "Vin Diesel XXXposed" [Pocket Books]*